Americans from Germany

by

GERARD WILK

Don Heinrich Tolzmann, *Editor*

MAX KADE GERMAN-AMERICAN CENTER
Indiana University-Purdue University at Indianapolis
and
INDIANA GERMAN HERITAGE SOCIETY, INC.
Indianapolis

MAX KADE GERMAN-AMERICAN CENTER
Indiana University-Purdue University at Indianapolis
and
INDIANA GERMAN HERITAGE SOCIETY, INC.
Deutsches Haus-Athenaeum, 401 East Michigan Street
Indianapolis, Indiana 46204

Eberhard Reichmann, *Editor-in-Chief*

Volume 7

Printed in the United States of America
by Fred Weidner & Son Printers, Inc.

Produced and distributed by
NCSA LITERATUR
430 S. Kelp Grove Road, Nashville, Indiana 47448

The Foreword to this volume is reprinted from *The German-Americans,*
by LaVern J. Rippley,
with permission of Twayne Publishers-K.K. Hall & Co., Boston.

Photo Credits: Rudolf Cronau, *Drei Jahrhunderte deutschen Lebens in
Amerika* (1924), for John Jacob Astor, Peter Muhlenberg, Carl Schurz,
Friedrich Wilhelm von Steuben; Bettman Archives for Ottmar
Mergenthaler and Robert Wagner Sr.; Berko of Aspen, Col. for Mies van
der Rohe. All other photos from German Information Center.

Table of Contents

*Picture

About This Reprint Edition (1995)

GERARD WILK's biographical sketches were first published in 1976 and reissued in 1987. His selection and the format he chose proved to be exceptionally useful both for instructional purposes and general information on prominent German-Americans who left their mark in the annals of American history.

The booklet was a little birthday gift to the nation's Bicentennial. The year-long observations and celebrations made 1976 a banner year of heritage consciousness, part of which was an unprecedented "ethnic revival" creating a new sense of historical identity—Roots. Within this context it was the first time since World War I days that the role German-Americans have been playing in U.S. history became a focal point of discussion in numerous publications, conferences, and exhibits.

Celebrating the German-American Tricentennial in 1983 and establishing October 6 as "German-American Day" in 1987 have since become key indicators of the significant national stature of German-Americana past and present. According to the 1990 U.S. Census, nearly one quarter of the population claims some form of German ancestry, thereby making the German-Americans the largest ethnic group. Since 1608, when the first permanent settlers at Jamestown, Virginia included some Germans, roughly eight million immigrants from German-speaking countries and regions arrived on American shores. They were not simply assimilated; they co-created the American way of life.

Despite numerous publications in the field of German-American Studies since 1976, Wilk's representative and handy biographical volume has never been replaced. We are grateful to Mrs. Gerard Wilk and the German Information Center New York for granting reprint permission.

We added President Reagan's "German-American Day, 1987: A Proclamation; " the German-American Heritage Map; German-American Census Statistics; and a "Selective Bibliography." Some of the original illustrations have been replaced.

April 1995
University of Cincinnati   Don Heinrich Tolzmann

Introduction

1976 was a most remarkable year for many reasons. The anniversary of a great nation, the bicentennial of the United States of America, was a major one of them; it has no less cheered the friends of America than it has her own citizens. Representing in the United States at this occasion a friendly country such as the Federal Republic of Germany has been an exhilarating experience. It will forever be among the most cherished episodes in my life as a diplomat. And I shall not cease to be grateful for the opportunity afforded me to see the long-standing good relations brought to new fruition, characterized by the remark of the President of the United States that "the relationship on a bilateral basis . . . could not be better."

In 1976, interaction between the United States and Germany has probably involved more people and was more frequent than ever before. Germans from all walks of life, individually and in groups, decided to discover and see for themselves the land of unlimited opportunities in which so many of their countrymen have succeeded — from its very beginning to the present day. They left behind a distinguished record of accomplishments and gave the best their native country had to contribute to a new nation, in which today twenty-five million profess to be of German ancestry.

German-Americans have added their share to the building of the United States of America. It is with pride and satisfaction that the people of a free and democratic Germany take note of this historic fact. The millions of nameless pioneers who crossed the Atlantic have made this country fertile while at the same time making a better living for themselves. Among them have always been people of outstanding ingenuity, skillfulness, courage or even statesmanship. Many of them are remembered; quite a few of them have left their imprints on the history of this country—and some of them came from Germany.

The endeavor to collect the biographies of at least some of them was spurred—like so many other projects—by the observance of the bicentennial year. The idea came from Dr. Gerard Wilk, himself a German-American—of the latest vintage of immigrants, who were as remarkable as those of the days of Carl Schurz: In seeking refuge from tyranny they added to the already tremendous spiritual wealth of America the very best of European humanism, art and science. Dr. Wilk's biographies "Americans from Germany" appeared successively in "Relay from Bonn," an Embassy publication released through the German Information Center in New York. It was felt subsequently that they should be made known to a larger public, for there seems to be no better way to remind us that relations between nations are made by people and consist of people — overcoming boundaries and bridging oceans.

Honoring in this Bicentennial Year some of those who have gained prominence in fostering German-American friendship—that is what this book is all about.

Berndt von Staden
Ambassador of the
Federal Republic of Germany

Foreword

The very success of the German immigrant in the United States — his tendency quickly to become part of American life as an individual, rather than as part of an ethnic group — has made it difficult to follow his tracks. Since the first escapees from oppressive rulers in the German princely states came to America before the Revolutionary War, German immigrants became enamored of the New World and became involved in the American scene around them. Genealogy was not their consuming passion; they became absorbed in their new communities. The story of the Germans in America and their distinctive contribution to our national development is an important component of the story of America.

We are becoming increasingly appreciative of the value of diversity in our national life. Each of the native strains that has come to our shores has made its contributions and left its mark. For all of us, life in America is a more thrilling experience because of this confluence of cultures.

We must not forget that when the United States was a developing country, it was on the receiving end of foreign aid. The most valuable foreign aid we received were the shiploads of immigrants who came to our shores, educated in European schools, trained in European concepts of religion, family life and civic order. The German immigrants were a valuable asset to this country from the day they arrived. They made immediate contributions to agriculture, commerce and industry. Some of them had achieved eminence in their own fields before they came to this hemisphere, and they brought with them the advanced technology and scholarship of the laboratories and universities of Europe. The dependence of American medicine and science on German roots is widely appreciated, but a similar situation prevails in many other fields — artistic, religious, manufacturing and commercial.

Students of American history are properly accustomed to associating the early British immigration with the search for freedom. This search was also true of the German immigrants. The Germans brought a liberal tradition to these shores and widely supported the Revolution. In 1848, when reactionary rulers in Berlin and Vienna suppressed attempts of liberals to implement constitutional reforms, thousands fled to America to escape arrest, and the United States was enriched by a remarkable group of men and women. They were violently opposed to slavery and to corrupt city political machines. And when they found freedom here, they encouraged their relatives in Germany to follow their examples. An 1847 letter from New York, distributed widely in Frankfurt, said, "Look across the Ocean. See the greatness, the flowering of our Republic. Try to govern yourselves. Don't let supercilious scholars throw dust in your eyes."

The German philosopher Johann Gottlieb Fichte, during the Napoleonic wars which forced many Germans to leave their homeland, wrote: "If nothing else, our best traditions might outlive us on fresh soil ... and the better side of a German culture might survive the perils of the present."

Time has proved the truth of this prediction.

Henry S. Reuss
Member of Congress
Fifth District, Wisconsin

German-American Day, 1987

By the President of the United States of America

A PROCLAMATION

MORE AMERICANS trace their heritage back to the German ancestry than to any other nationality. More than seven million Germans have come to our shores through the years, and today some 60 million Americans—one in four—are of German descent. Few people have blended so completely into the multicultural tapestry of American society and yet have made such singular economic, political, social, scientific, and cultural contributions to the growth and success of these United States as have Americans of German extraction.

The United States has embraced a vast array of German traditions, institutions, and influences. Many of these have become so accepted as parts of our way of life that their ethnic origin has been obscured. For instance, Christmas trees and Broadway musicals are familiar features of American society. Our kindergartens, graduate schools, the social security system, and labor unions are all based on models derived from Germany.

German teachers, musicians, and enthusiastic amateurs have left an indelible imprint on classical music, hymns, choral singing, and marching bands in our country. In architecture and design, German contributions include the modern suspension bridge, Bauhaus, and Jugendstil. German-American scientists have helped make the United States the world's pioneer in research and technology. The American work ethic, a major factor in the rapid rise of the United States to preeminence in agriculture and industry, owes much to German-Americans' commitment to excellence.

For more than three centuries, Germans have helped build, invigorate, and strengthen this country. But the United States has given as well as received. Just a generation ago, America conceived of and swiftly implemented the Marshall Plan, which helped the new German democracy rise from the rubble of war to become a beacon of democracy in Central Europe. The Berlin Airlift demonstrated the

American commitment to the defense of freedom when, still recovering from the war, Berlin was threatened by strangulation from the Soviets.

Today, the Federal Republic of Germany is a bulwark of democracy in the heart of a divided Europe. Germans and Americans are rightfully proud of our common values as well as our shared heritage. For more than three decades the German-American partnership has been a linchpin in the Western Alliance. Thanks to it, a whole generation of Americans and Europeans has grown up free to enjoy the fruits of liberty.

Our histories are thus intertwined. We now contribute to each other's trade, enjoy each other's cultures, and learn from each other's experiences. The German-American Friendship Garden, which will be dedicated in the District of Columbia in the near future, is symbolic of the close and amicable relations between West Germany and the United States.

The Congress, by Public Law 100-104, has designated October 6, 1987, the 304th anniversary of the arrival of the first German immigrants in Philadelphia, as "German-American Day" and has authorized and requested the President to issue a proclamation in observance of that day.

NOW, THEREFORE, I, RONALD REAGAN, President of the United States of America, do hereby proclaim Tuesday, October 6, 1987, as German-American Day. I urge all Americans to learn more about the contributions of German immigrants to the life and culture of the United States and to observe this day with appropriate ceremonies and activities.

IN WITNESS WHEREOF, I have hereunto set my hand this second day of October, in the year of our Lord nineteen hundred and eighty- seven, and of the Independence of the United States of America the two hundred and twelfth.

Ronald Reagan

Josef and Anni Albers

The example of Josef Albers (born in Bottrop in 1888) and of his wife Anni (born in Berlin in 1899) shows that the extraordinary influence that the Bauhaus has had in America was by no means limited to the field of architecture. Josef Albers, painter, philosopher, teacher and writer, taught at the Bauhaus in Dessau from 1923 until its dissolution in 1933. The ascetic discipline of his paintings on glass of that time "created a new language in painting." (Eugen Grominger) "Since his days at the Bauhaus, Albers pursued one and the same idea — to grasp and understand the world through images, from a visual perspective." (Will Grohman)

In his paintings and graphic designs, which made him famous after his emigration to America — and among which the series "Homage to the Square" has become the best known — Albers "rejected accidental effects and limited emotional factors to a minimum." (Ruth Gilbert) As a teacher, Albers was of uncommon importance in the United States too. He taught at Black Mountain College in North Carolina and later at Yale University, where he became Dean of the School of Architecture and Design. Among other things, Albers is considered a forerunner of Op Art.

Albers was a member of the National Institute of Art and Letters and in 1968 was awarded the Commander's Cross of the Order of Merit of the Federal Republic of Germany.

Anni Albers, who also taught at the Bauhaus — from 1922 to 1930 — and later at American universities, became known as a pioneer of art weaving. In 1959 she published "On Designing," and "On Weaving" followed in 1965.

Josef Albers' paintings and graphic works are exhibited by many European and American museums, including the Metropolitan Museum of Art, the Museum of Modern Art and the Whitney Museum in New York. He died on March 25th 1976 at the age of 88.

John Peter Altgeld

According to the poet Vachel Lindsay, John Peter Altgeld, Governor of Illinois from 1892 to 1896, is recorded in the annals of America's social reform movement as "an eagle forgotten who kindled the flame, who served the wretched, the deprived, the lame and the poor. ..."

Born in Nieder Selters in Hesse on December 30, 1847, he was very young when he arrived in America with his parents who then went to work on a farm near Mansfield, Ohio. At age sixteen, Altgeld volunteered for the Civil War and later wandered through Missouri and Arkansas as an itinerant worker. A self-taught man, he became a teacher, studied law, and became an attorney for poor people in Chicago, and served as a judge. In 1884, he published a book on prison reform which gained him many enemies and which remains topical today.

An alliance of Democrats and the United Labor Party assured his election as governor. His appointment of Florence Kelly, who attempted to prohibit child labor, and his draft bill requiring inspection of sanitary conditions in factories, made him unpopular among the city's powerful industrialists. After pardoning three anarchists who had been sentenced to life in prison for the Haymarket bombing (four had already been executed), he became known as John "Pardon" Altgeld. Although many people had demanded the pardon, by granting it Altgeld branded the trial, the prosecution, the judge, and the jury as biased. Altgeld's action produced strong protest. Actually the guilt of the defendants had never been proven.

In 1894, there was a militant strike against the Pullman factories in Chicago. President Cleveland, at the instigation of the Attorney General, Richard Olney, responded by sending in federal troops. Governor Altgeld protested sharply against this violation of state's rights. He knew what Cleveland might not have known—that Olney, one of the founders of the General Managers' Association, wanted to make an example of this case, which resulted in the death of more than twelve persons. J.T. Adams writes in The Epic of America that (unconsciously) "Cleveland played into the hands of the railroad owners."

With this incident, Altgeld's political career was over. A broken man, he returned to being a defender of the poor. He died on March 11, 1902. The famous defense lawyer, Clarence Darrow, eulogized him as follows: "Even his admirers have probably never understood the true nature of this great humanist. . . . Like all great souls, he was a solitary man . . . For him life was an endless tragedy—the earth was a great hospital full of the sick, the wounded and the suffering, and he devoted himself to them like a dedicated surgeon. . . . "

John Jacob Astor

John Jacob Astor, who was born on July 17, 1763, and whose name was later to appear in the names of cities, boroughs, places and hotels, was the first of the legendary "self-made men." With only seven flutes in his possession, he arrived in New York in March of 1784 to follow his brother Henry who was selling meat at the flea market. At his death on March 29, 1848, as the richest man in America, he left his second son a fortune of 20 million dollars.

His original plan was to open a musical instruments shop, but his first job was as delivery-boy for a bakery (a memory that he always repressed later). Then he became an assistant in a furrier's shop. The owner, Robert Bowe, repeatedly sent him northward into the wilderness with heavy baggage on his back — going out were cheap gifts for the Indians, coming back were costly pelts. Soon Astor went into business on his own, financed by the 300 dollar dowry of his wife, Sarah Todd, who came from a well-respected family. Then Astor dealt in furs and pianos. Soon there were only furs, which he exported to London and later to China. He made his first million by 1810.

John Adams, second President of the United States, deplored that "moneyed nobility is our aristocracy." Astor became the most influential representative of this aristocracy. During President Jefferson's Embargo he could even afford to deceive the President and use a trick to send his ship, the "Beaver," to China — at a net profit of 200,000 dollars. But when he founded Astoria on the Columbia River (which proved to be a losing deal) in what is today Oregon, Jefferson thanked him: "I consider the establishment of settlements on the North-West coast a public benefit . . ."

Even though Astoria was occupied by the English in 1812, Astor had become "the Czar of the fur trade in the Northwest where his power was greater than that of the Government." (J. T. Adams in "The Epic of America.") In 1834, he sold off all his fur interests and devoted himself exclusively to real estate speculation and was soon known as the "landlord of New York."

From 1837 until 1840, Astor was an active President of the Deutsche Gesellschaft (German Society) which aided poor immigrants, and also presented the society with a handsome endowment. In his will, he left $400,000 for the establishment of the Astor Library on Lafayette Street, where Joseph Papp today has his Public Thea-

JOHN JACOB ASTOR

ter) which was the nucleus of the later New York Public Library. In his hometown, he founded an orphanage.

No history of New York and hardly any history of the United States, ignores his powerful personality. Admiration for his achievements is usually mixed with criticism of his ruthless methods, which, however, differed little from those of the other great entrepreneurs of his era. One fact is always emphasized — in his private life, too, Astor practiced thrift and was a faithful provider and family man. He loved music and theater. He did not care for the old-line New York patricians who rejected him, but he was received by the kings and aristocrats of Europe. Until his death, he maintained a close friendship with the poet Washington Irving, who wrote the fascinating story of Astor's creation, "Astoria."

Albert Bierstadt

Albert Bierstadt (born in Solingen on January 7, 1830; died in New York on February 18, 1920) was one of the most prominent painters on two continents during the sixties and seventies of the previous century. Having grown up in Bedford, Massachusetts, Bierstadt returned to Duesseldorf at the age of 23 to study at the Academy of Arts under Andreas Achenbach and Karl Friedrich Lessing.

In 1859, Bierstadt joined General Lander's expedition to the Rocky Mountains and became the first man to paint the snow-covered high country, the granite domes and cathedrals of the Sierra Nevada and the Yosemite Valley. "I found," wrote Bierstadt, "the figures of the Indians and their picturesque dress very alluring. Their customs and habits are still the same as they were hundreds of years ago—now is the time to paint them for they are disappearing fast." Bierstadt made paintings and drawings which, in addition to their artistic significance, are of a documentary value that continues to be highly esteemed.

His powerful, even outsized landscapes portraying the wild grandeur of virgin country and the loneliness of the Indians who were often shown standing forlornly in the foreground (such as "Landers Peak" and "Storm in the Rocky Mountains," "Evening on Mount Tacoma," and "Indian Camp at the Base of the Rocks") quickly gained him fame, remuneration, and high honors, including the French Legion of Honor and the Gold Medal at an exhibition of the

WERNHER VON BRAUN

Berlin Academy. Bierstadt's paintings appealed to a romantic longing for the wild West among his contemporaries.

𝔚𝔢𝔯𝔫𝔥𝔢𝔯 𝔟𝔬𝔫 𝔅𝔯𝔞𝔲𝔫

The name Wernher von Braun (born March 23, 1912 in what is now the Polish town of Wirsitz) is inseparably connected with American space flight and with the moon landing. His interest in astronomy was stimulated from an early age by his mother. As a mathematical prodigy, von Braun was profoundly impressed by Hermann Oberth's book "Rockets to Interplanetary Space" published in 1923, and became committed to space travel. In 1932, he entered the ordinance corps of the army at the suggestion of Captain Walter Dornberger. He was awarded his degree in 1934 in Berlin. With the participation of a group under his direction, he succeeded in that same year in firing the first two rockets vertically for a distance greater than a mile. For the purpose of carrying out further research, his team was transferred from Berlin to Peenemuende, where von Braun constructed the V-2 rockets. In 1945, he and his co-workers surrendered to the Americans, and approximately 120 emigrated to America.

Von Braun had married his cousin Marie Louise von Quistorp in 1947 while still in Germany; the move to Huntsville, Alabama, took place in 1950 (neighbors spoke of Sauerkraut Hill). In 1953, the first short-distance rocket, the Redstone, came into being. The surprise launching of Sputnik I on October 4, 1957, caused great excitement, and von Braun promised, on condition that he receive the necessary support, to put an earth satellite into orbit within a few months. With Explorer I, which was launched on January 31, 1958, he kept his word.

As Director of the George C. Marshall Space Center under the auspices of the newly established NASA, von Braun created Saturn I, IB, and the largest of the 3-stage thrust rockets, Saturn V. Saturn V made possible the first Apollo moon landing. Von Braun, having become an American citizen in 1955, was transferred to Washington. He later resigned from his position there and joined Fairchild Industries as Vice President for Development. He received high commendations from the American government and from scientific societies and was awarded twenty honorary doctorates. The Mars Project (published in 1952) may be mentioned as just one of his many publications.

Von Braun "is one of the pioneers in the historic adventure in the conquest of space. He held a key position in the first chapter of the dramatic contest with the Russian competition" (Christine Totten: Deutschland Soll und Haben). Von Braun is known for his sense of humor and once said of himself, "I am a two-headed monster, a scientist and a public relations man." As his biographer Bergaust explains, he needed both talents in order to land the first Americans on the moon.

𝔄𝔡𝔬𝔩𝔭𝔥𝔲𝔰 𝔅𝔲𝔰𝔠𝔥

The families Anheuser and Busch, the principal owners today of the far-flung brewery and industrial concern, have been closely connected with the company of Anheuser-Busch since the middle of the last century. In 1857, the German immigrant Eberhard Anheuser assumed ownership of a Bavarian brewery that was heavily indebted to him.

In 1857, Adolphus Busch had come to St. Louis from Mainz, where his father was in the wine business. He fought in the Union Army during the Civil War. At the end of the war, he took over the direction of the brewery, and in this capacity came into contact with Anheuser. The firm of Anheuser-Busch, producers of Budweiser Beer, dates from 1870. Beer production increased from 3000 barrels in 1865 to 700,000 barrels in 1870.

Adolphus Busch became a legendary figure in St. Louis as a successful businessman (he was the first to have refrigerated railroad cars built in order to be able to ship beer to distant points) and as a patron of the arts and host who entertained Europe's elite (among them, Edward VII of England) in his castle on the Rhine. Having witnessed the San Francisco earthquake on April 17, 1906, he initiated a vast aid program to which he sent $100,000 as his contribution. With his son-in-law, Hugo Reisinger (husband of Edmee Busch), he founded Harvard University's Busch-Reisinger Museum of Germanic Culture. Busch died on October 11, 1911. His principles, including the spirit of philanthropy, are carried on by grandson, Gert von Gontard, who has been the principal force behind the German Theater, Inc., in New York, since 1946.

Albert Einstein

Albert Einstein (born March 14, 1879 in Ulm), the originator of the theory of relativity, is regarded as one of the most important scientists of the modern era. As a 26-year old technical expert at the patent office in Bern, he wrote three treatises that revolutionized physics. He extended Max Planck's quantum theory, and his Special Theory of Relativity became of fundamental importance for subsequent developments in modern physics. His General Theory of Relativity, published in 1915, attempted a more comprehensive explanation of the principle of relativity and provided new postulates concerning cosmology and space exploration. Although these findings were regarded as too revolutionary to be recognized by the Nobel Prize Committee, he was awarded the Nobel Prize in 1921 for his work in the fields of photoelectricity and theoretical physics.

Even as a boy, he was attracted by abstract thinking. In a short autobiography, written at age 67, that he called his necrologue, he stated, "As a precocious young man, I came to the conclusion from reading popular scientific books that much contained in Bible stories could not be true, with the result that I absolutely became a freethinker and moreover had the impression that the state intentionally lied to youth. The effect was shattering, and as a result of this experience I was mistrustful of every kind of authority..." Einstein nonetheless remained throughout his life a deeply religious person, free of all dogma. He repeatedly stressed the belief that "God does not gamble with the universe."

Einstein's interests were by no means limited to mathematics and physics. He published philosophical writings and actively supported numerous humanitarian causes such as the League of Nations and the anti-war movement.

After 1913, he served as director of the highly esteemed Kaiser-Wilhelm-Institut for Physics in Berlin, and after 1914 as a member of the Prussian Academy of Sciences.

In 1933, his house was seized. He renounced his German

citizenship and membership in the Prussian Academy. He found refuge in Princeton, New Jersey, where he became director of the mathematics faculty of the newly founded Institute for Advanced Studies and Princeton's most popular inhabitant. "The mere presence of Einstein was of overwhelming importance to America. His was the only familiar name among all the immigrants who came to America, and he became the symbol of persecuted European intellectuals," according to Laura Fermi, widow of the atomic physicist Enrico Fermi, in "Illustrious Immigrants."

Despite his international fame and popularity, Einstein lived very modestly with his family in Princeton. He was a special favorite among children there, and one Christmas evening as they were singing Christmas carols in front of his house, he asked, "Should I accompany you?" He then took his violin and made the rounds with them in the cold.

Events in Germany oppressed him greatly. "I am a resolute but not an absolute pacifist," he said. In the year 1939, months before the outbreak of World War II, the physicists Eugene Wigner and Leo Szilard, who also lived in Princeton, visited him to inform him that German attempts at splitting the atom could soon lead to production of an atomic bomb. They were convinced that Hitler wanted war and that Einstein should accordingly warn President Roosevelt, since he was considered to be the only one among them to whom the White House would listen. After long hesitation, Einstein decided on August 2, 1939 to send the President the memorandum that Szilard had already written along with an accompanying letter of his own through an emissary. The warning was heeded, but while the first atomic bomb was being built at Los Alamos, Einstein was told nothing about the project.

After the war, he regarded a world government as the only hope for saving mankind from atomic death, and he worked for its realization. In 1952, Israel invited him to be the successor of their first president, Chaim Weizmann, who had just died. Einstein declined the honor.

Albert Einstein died April 18, 1955, in Princeton.

Karl Follen

Dr. Karl Follen (born Follenius on September 4, 1796 in Giessen) was a jurist, educator, poet, and in his later years a minister. He was one of the first Germans in America to gain a profound influence on the American liberal spirit. As an unswerving liberal, Follen was the spokesman of Germans whose enthusiastic enlistment in the war against Napoleon had been followed by disappointment under the reactionary measures of Metternich. Follen had become the acknowledged leader of the "Blacks, or the Resolutes," a university fraternity whose goal was to fight for a united Germany. Its banner song, "Down with Crowns and Thrones! Storm the Gates! Brothers, Storm the Gates!" (Nieder mit Kronen und Thronen! Sturm, Ihr Brueder zum Sturm!), was the forbidden hymn of the rebels.

Realizing the impossibility of effecting change in Germany, Follen wrote a pamphlet advocating mass emigration to the prairies of North America for the purpose of establishing German republics to be used as a stepping-stone toward revolution in the homeland. The pamphlet was seized by the police. Follen subsequently became innocently involved in the trial of Karl Ludwig Sand, the assassin of the writer and alleged traitor August von Kotzebue. Follen was imprisoned, but fled to Switzerland, where he taught until residence was denied him at the instigation of the Prussian authorities. In Paris he obtained a letter of safe conduct from the Marquis de Lafayette and sailed for New York on November 1, 1824. He soon realized that his plan for German republics in America was impossible. Although he publicized his revised views in Germany, his initial goal of establishing German states in America continued to find adherents in Germany.

The first German academic chair in America was established for Follen by Harvard University. On September 15, 1828, he married Eliza Lee Cabot (August 15, 1787–January 26, 1860) from the well-known Boston patrician family. Boston's Brahmins accepted Follen, only to turn against him again soon thereafter. Follen supported liberation of the slaves with inflammatory zeal and, among other things, wrote a pamphlet, "Address to the American People," which was widely distributed and whose tone resembled the appeal to the German Pietists in Germantown of the year 1688. In January 1836, Follen appeared before the Massachusetts legislature in support of abolition. "As long as I live, as a good American, as a good

German, and as a good Christian, I will fight for the cause of the liberation of Negroes." Harvard dismissed him, and a new life of wandering began. At the instigation of his wife, he became a preacher in the Unitarian Church, and he was to take up his duties in that capacity at a meagerly paid independent congregation in East Lexington on January 15, 1840. After giving lectures in New York he took a boat back to Boston, which sank in an ice floe on Long Island on January 13, 1840. Follen was not among the four survivors.

𝕸𝖆𝖓𝖋𝖗𝖊𝖉 𝕲𝖊𝖔𝖗𝖌𝖊

Manfred George (born in Berlin on October 23, 1893) founded the German-Jewish weekly, Aufbau, which is published in New York. The Aufbau emerged from an immigrant newsletter to become a newspaper with a world-wide circulation.

After being severely wounded in World War I, George studied under the famous criminal legal specialist, Franz von Liszt, and was awarded the doctorate in Berlin in 1919. He subsequently became a successful journalist with the Ullstein Publishing House, was appointed editor-in-chief of the Berliner Abendpost, and in 1928 editor-in-chief of the newly-founded evening paper, Tempo. His biographies of Walter Rathenau, Theodor Herzl, Carl Sternheim, and Marlene Dietrich were widely read. He worked as editor-in-chief of the Prager Morgenzeitung in Czechoslovakia before coming to the United States.

In 1939, he was appointed editor of the Aufbau in New York. The paper, which then consisted of only a few pages, soon became the main forum of the "other Germany" for German immigrants, both Jewish and non-Jewish.

Despite George's militancy during the war, he was among the first to resume communications with Germany after the war ended, and soon thereafter became a contributor to publications in the Federal Republic. George also gave valuable support to the emerging off-Broadway theater.

When George died on December 30, 1965, the Federal Chancellor, Ludwig Erhard, commented: "The death of Manfred George deeply affects all who, like me, grew up during the flowering of German journalism. Manfred George was an important journalist, an honorable man who always worked to build bridges between the

German emigration and the country of his origin. We remember him gratefully."

Walter Gropius

"We have all studied at the Bauhaus," states Newsweek (December 15, 1969). Walter Gropius (born May 18, 1883 in Berlin) founded the Bauhaus in Weimar in 1919. After 1925, he moved it to Dessau, where it made its most important contributions. Gropius was one of the architects who "led the character and ideals of American building onto another path," according to a publication by the Museum of Modern Art. The influence of the Bauhaus extended to the visual arts, including stage scenery, furniture, textile and industrial design.

Even before World War I, Gropius advocated the use of prefabricated construction elements. Like his colleague, Mies van der Rohe, Gropius taught his students to have regard for skill and craftsmanship. He adhered to his fundamental aim of "giving a soul to the lifeless product of the machine." As early as 1911, his Fagus factory in Alfeld attracted the attention of architects all over the world. His building for the Bauhaus in Dessau is considered a monument of modern architectural design.

In 1928, Gropius returned to Berlin as an independent architect and built a housing complex in the Siemensstadt settlement. In 1934, he emigrated to London. In 1937, he was appointed to teach at the School of Architecture of Harvard University. He served as Dean of the School of Architecture for many years until his retirement in 1952. In 1946, Gropius founded the Architects' Collaborative with his students. Until his death on July 5, 1969, he remained a member of the Collaborative, which worked strictly as a team both in carrying out work assignments and in sharing remuneration.

Oscar Hammerstein I

Oscar Hammerstein (born in Berlin on May 8, 1847, although the date is disputed) was the founder of six opera companies in the U.S. His dream was to build an opera house in every major American city. He has been called "the German-American impresario who brought

WALTER GROPIUS

many important singers and prima-donnas to America, who earned millions and sacrificed them to his passion for opera and who did not care about money.'' He repeatedly said of himself: 'I am the man of the street who brings opera to the masses.'' He did so by engaging such singers as Mary Garden, Luisa Tetrazzini, Lina Cavallieri, Nellie Melba, Marcel Renaud, Allesandro Bonci, John McCormack. Hammerstein also wanted a people's opera house — and the Metropolitan Opera was his implacable enemy. Flamboyant, tough, feared and loved, his picture appeared in the press often and his name filled the headlines for decades.

The oldest of five children from a respectable family, Hammerstein ran away from home at the age of sixteen, sold his violin, and sailed to New York in steerage. He learned to roll cigars, listened to ''Martha'' and other German operas in a beer hall, became friendly with the German choir master Adolf Neuendorff and believed that he had to ''produce operas or die.'' Patents for merchandizing the production of cigars at a good selling price made it possible for him in 1889 to build the Harlem Opera. In doing so, he exceeded his resources, but the great Lilly Lehmann helped him out of the financial difficulty. Fortune's wheel always spun very quickly for Hammerstein. Opera houses were erected, including the Manhattan Opera in 1906 and others in London and Philadalphia, but in 1910 he had to give up in his battle against the ''Met.'' As a lover of serious opera, it was with great inner reluctance that he produced the musical ''Naughty Marietta'' with Emma Trentini.

Hammerstein died on August, 1919 in Lenox Hill Hospital. ''His statue should be erected in Times Square,'' Carl van Vechten wrote. To date that has not been done. His grandson, the lyricist Oscar Hammerstein II (''Oklahoma'') became co-author of America's most popular Broadway musicals.

Friedrich Hecker

Friedrich Hecker, (born in Eichtersheim on September 28, 1811), who appealed to the Frankfurt Assembly for a German Republic and German unity, was a popular figure in the German uprising of 1848. His popularity in America was by no means restricted to German immigrants, and more than 20,000 New Yorkers welcomed him in a sea of black-red-gold banners when he arrived in December of 1848

15

to raise funds for the continuation of the struggle. Even though he had been defeated at Kandern, he was honored as if he were a victor. On April 12, 1848, he had called for a popular uprising in Konstanz, expecting that tens of thousands would join his march for freedom, following the example of peasant uprisings. Only 75 responded, however, and he marched with them. He proudly observed, "I always went alone, whether someone came along or not."

Hecker again returned to Germany, but only reached Strassbourg, because the course of the German revolution had come to an end at Rastatt.

Unlike most of the Forty-Eighters, Hecker did not remain in a city, but bought a farm in Summerfield near Belleville, Illinois and prospered. He remained active intellectually and politically, gave lectures, founded the Turnverein in Cincinnati, played a significant role in the founding of the Republican Party and in the election of Lincoln, and was strongly committed to the cause of abolition.

At the outbreak of the Civil War, he and his son volunteered. He first served as a private under General Sigel, who had come from Baden. He was subsequently appointed colonel and commanded the 24th Illinois Infantry regiment, a position he resigned after differences with his superiors. He was then commissioned to recruit the 82nd Illinois Regiment, using his own funds in part for the purpose, which he commanded long and successfully. Hecker was severely wounded at Chancellorsville. In 1873, he paid a visit to his hometown, where he was welcomed with torchlight processions and shadowed by the police. Although he was asked to remain, he did not. Hecker died on his farm on March 24, 1881.

Abraham Jacobi

Dr. Abraham Jacobi, father of American pediatrics gave his name to the city hospital in the Bronx, New York. He was and remained a lifelong Forty-Eighter. As a student (he was awarded his degree by Bonn University in 1851), he had fought on the barricades, been imprisoned in Berlin, Bielefeld, and Cologne and escaped from prison in Minden in 1853. Born in Hartum/Westfalia on May 6, 1830, the son of poor Jewish parents, he was a champion of the poor. Upon the suggestion of his friend, Carl Schurz, he opened a practice in New York City's Howard Street, where he treated patients for 25 cents.

Jacobi specialized in pediatrics, a branch of medicine then new in America, and gained an international reputation through his publications. In 1860, he was appointed to be the first Professor of Pediatrics at the New York Medical College. From 1870 until 1902, he taught as Professor of Pediatrics at the City University of New York and in close cooperation with the charitable German Society of the city of New York, he was a co-founder of the Association of Doctors for the Poor, and of the German Dispensary, which later became Lenox Hill Hospital. There and at Mount Sinai Hospital, Jacobi established the first children's wards.

On July 22, 1873, he married Mary Corinna Putnam, also a well-known doctor, whose ancestors had been early Puritan settlers.

In 1894, Jacobi declined an invitation to teach at the University of Berlin.

Despite some protest because of his advocacy of family planning and of laws prohibiting child labor, Jacobi was elected President of the American Medical Association at age 82. No other foreign-born doctor had ever been so honored.

The Jacobis owned a summer house on Lake George next to the property of their friend, Carl Schurz. When their house containing some still unpublished manuscripts burned, the 89-year-old Jacobi was unable to recover sufficiently from the shock to attend ceremonies planned for his 90th birthday. He died on July 10, 1919, in the New York apartment of Carl Schurz.

Johann de Kalb

Military history places Johann de Kalb (who was born in Huettendorf in Bavaria on June 29, 1721) among Washington's most able generals. He was a self-made military man whose parents were peasants. De Kalb joined the French Army and the Alsatian and Lothringian Regiment of Count Loewendal and fought numerous campaigns in the Seven Years' War. He was made colonel, assumed an aristocratic title that was confirmed in 1763, married the wealthy Anne de Robais, became an intimate of the influential Comte de Broglie, and gained entrance to the most exclusive circles of Paris.

In 1768, he was sent to America to report to pro-American French groups on growing tensions in the British colonies. He foresaw future developments clearly, and was forced to leave

America when the English intercepted his correspondence with the Duke of Choiseul.

He then returned to his estate of Milon-la-Chapelle near Versailles. For professional and political reasons, he was determined to assist the Americans, a goal shared by the Marquis de Layfayette, whose mentor de Kalb became. Through the intercession of the American envoy in Paris at de Kalb's behest, the 19-year-old Lieutenant Lafayette was made an American Major General, a fact that subsequently became important in French support for the American cause.

In America, de Kalb himself, even though occasionally confronted by hostility toward foreigners, was given several field commands. The three attacks led by him at age 59 in an attempt to relieve Camden, South Carolina, have often been depicted in words and paintings as proof of his great courage. On August 19, 1780, he succumbed to many severe wounds. Congress erected a memorial to de Kalb in Annapolis. In 1825, Lafayette laid the cornerstone for a statue in memory of him in Camden. The inscription on the statue reads: "German by birth, cosmopolitan by principle, his love of freedom made him help the citizens of the New World in their fight for independence." Counties in several states have been named for de Kalb.

Henry A. Kissinger

Of the many millions who came from Germany to America, perhaps no one has had a greater opportunity directly to shape the destiny of his new homeland than Henry A. Kissinger, the first German-born U.S. Secretary of State.

Heinz Alfred Kissinger was born on May 27, 1923, in the Bavarian town of Fuerth where his father taught at a girls' secondary school. Growing up in an orthodox Jewish family, he became a good, if not outstanding student, with a pronounced love of soccer, that he still retains. Even then, childhood friends report, his game was one of strategy rather than force.

After Hitler came to power in 1933, the family was subjected to increasing discrimination. The father was deprived of his job and soon the family was forced to join the millions of refugees from Nazi persecution. Louis and Paula Kissinger and their two sons arrived in

New York City in 1938. For Heinz, now Henry, the change meant night classes at City College and work during the day in a factory. In 1943, Kissinger was drafted into the U.S. Army. After 1945, he became a district administrator with the military government in the American-occupied zone of Germany.

Having taught at the Army's European Command Intelligence School, he returned to the U.S. in 1946 and entered Harvard College as a government major on a New York State scholarship. There he was elected to Phi Beta Kappa. He wrote so ambitious a senior honors thesis—on Kant, Spengler, and Toynbee—that the school decided to adopt a 'Kissinger rule' limiting the efforts of future students to 150 pages.

Kissinger was to remain at Harvard for most of the next 19 years, earning his Ph.D. in 1954 with an outstanding dissertation later published as 'A World Restored; Castlereagh, Metternich, and the Problems of Peace.'

As executive director of Harvard's foreign student project (later Harvard International Seminar), he established close contacts with many future leaders from all over the world.

While still at Harvard, he also worked on a study for the Council on Foreign Relations ('Nuclear Weapons and Foreign Policy') and served as advisor in various capacities to Presidents Eisenhower, Kennedy, and Johnson. Nelson Rockefeller, whom Kissinger had met through the council, sought him out as advisor and friend. The transition from academic life to political action became complete in 1969, when Kissinger was appointed Assistant to the President for National Security Affairs. He revitalized the National Security Council and shaped it into a major force in American foreign policy. He then had the opportunity to exercise his diplomatic skills, winning praise from Soviet Ambassador Dobrynin for being able to 'eat caviar with chopsticks.'

Broad new initiatives became his trademark — the opening moves toward Peking, the easing of relations with the Soviet Union, in particular the conclusion of the first agreement on the limitation of strategic arms (SALT), the ending of the conflict in Vietnam, and the successful 'shuttle diplomacy' in the Middle East. He was appointed Secretary of State in 1973. The Nobel Peace Prize in the same year recognized his efforts for international peace and stability.

As a man in politics, Kissinger has not been spared controversy. But he has also always known that 'the necessity of choice' makes this inevitable. As John G. Stoessinger, Professor of Political Science

HENRY A. KISSINGER

at the City University of New York, wrote recently: 'When history makes its judgment of the foreign policy of Henry Kissinger, the chronicle will not, Kissinger feels, pay much attention to his personal anguish when he was forced to choose between competing claims. Its iron pen will merely register the objective consequences of his acts. Nor will history reveal alternatives had he acted otherwise. He will never know where the road not taken might have led. The unending quest for meaningful choices in a tragic world in which the only certainty is risk, simply is a statesman's lot. It is therefore, in action in the present that courage and humanity are born.'

𝔍𝔞𝔨𝔬𝔟 𝔏𝔢𝔦𝔰𝔩𝔢𝔯

Lieutenant Governor Jakob Leisler, originally from Frankfort-on-Main, was hanged by the British in Manhattan on May 16, 1691. Thus the Leisler Rebellion officially ended, although the effects endured for a long time, and the controversy about Leisler's attitude and personality still persists. Most historians agree, however, on two points — that Leisler, as the first to summon the colonies to joint action not dictated from London, paved the way for the congress that met 88 years later and hence was a pioneer of American independence; and it was Leisler who "split the electorate into two parties, a party for the people and a party for the patricians, and thus made it impossible for the governors to rule the colonies according to whim. . . . " (E. R. Ellis: The Epic of New York)

New York and Leisler were involved in England's Glorious Revolution, which removed the Catholic James II from the throne and brought the Protestant Prince William of Orange to power. Protestant New York feared popery as did Leisler, who had been baptized as a Calvinist on May 31, 1640, as the son of a Calvinist minister who had to leave the Palatinate because of his belief. New Yorkers also feared that the French would attack and seize their militarily unprotected colonies since the great English dispute between Catholicism and Protestantism was simultaneously the beginning of the second Hundred Years War between England and Catholic France (May 7, 1689), which was carried on in the New World as the French and Indian Wars.

In the turbulence, Leisler played a significant role. He had come to New Amsterdam as a 20-year-old corporal in the service of

Holland. He turned to fur-trading, became rich, and was very wealthy when he married the widow of Pieter van der Veens (April, 1663). He was soon regarded as one of the most affluent New Yorkers and became deacon of the Dutch Reform Church and a senior captain of the New York militia. He was surrounded by poor people. Although he was related through marriage to the most highly placed patricians, he was rejected by them. The Governor had fled, and the new governor appointed by King William, Lieutenant Henry Sloughter, arrived only in the spring of 1691. The French and Indians pressed ahead and in those circumstances Leisler's actions resulted in bloody disputes in New York. On May 1, 1690, Leisler called upon the colonies to unite in defense, and for that he was never forgiven.

In the subsequent trial for high treason, the party of the aristocrats pressed for a death sentence, which Sloughter approved after having been made drunk at a banquet. There were tumultuous scenes at the execution. His enemies wanted to buy his heart from the hangman, and his supporters attempted to demonstrate in protest. In 1695, the Parliament in London rescinded the judgement and Leisler's confiscated wealth was returned to the family. A monument was erected to Leisler by the town of New Rochelle, where he owned property. In 1974, Pace University, whose campus includes the site of the execution, dedicated a memorial plaque to him in the presence of his American descendants.

Emanuel Leutze

"Washington Crossing the Delaware" is the most often reproduced painting in America (A.H. Hutton: "Portrait of Patriotism"). The artist, Emanuel Gottlieb Leutze, was born in Schwaebisch-Gmuend on May 24, 1816, grew up in Fredericksburg, Virginia, and created the painting in 1851, in Duesseldorf where he had gone to study. His parents had emigrated to America in 1825 for religious reasons. The father, a silversmith who had owned his own factory, managed in America only with difficulty and died in 1831.

Emanuel's portraits attracted attention even as a ten-year-old, and his painting, "Indians Looking at the Setting Sun," enabled him to go abroad and study at the Art Academy in Duesseldorf, where he met the painter Albert Bierstadt, who also was originally from Germany and had grown up in America. They became friends and shared the wish "of paying dramatic tribute to their new homeland on canvas."

"The First Landing of the Normans in America" brought Leutze fame in Germany that extended to America. Painting upon painting followed, often with life-size figures, such as "The Settlement of Maryland" and "Columbus' Festive Reception upon his First Return from America." Leutze became famous as the painter of two worlds exemplified by "Washington in Monmouth" and "Crown Prince Friedrich II's Return from Spandau." The first version of "Washington's Crossing" which was restored after suffering damage in a gallery fire, is the property of the Kunsthalle in Bremen; the second version hangs in the Metropolitan Museum of New York.

In 1859, Leutze returned to America, crowned with gold medals from both continents and bearing the title of professor conferred by the King of Prussia. He was commissioned to decorate the House of Representatives in Washington. For this purpose, he undertook long, difficult journeys into unexplored areas and into Indian territory, which resulted in "Westward the Course of Empire Takes its Way," wherein Leutze combined realistic Western landscapes with an allegorical portrayal of settlements on the borders of civilization. Leutze died suddenly in Washington on July 18, 1868, while at work on "Abolition of Slavery," another painting intended for the Capitol.

"Leutze introduced into America the sentimental realism of German historical painting," says the Oxford Companion to Art. "He thereby attained extraordinary popularity in America for many decades..."

Francis Lieber

Francis Lieber was the first German political scientist who was to gain a lasting influence on intellectual life in America. In Boston he founded the Encyclopedia Americana — the first of its kind in the United States — and created the foundations for modern martial law. His works such as "Manual of Political Ethics," "Civil Liberty and Self-Government," and "Penal Laws and the Penitentiary System," as well as his textbooks were widely used for decades. Like Charles Follen and Carl Schurz, Lieber was a German revolutionary and patriot but only America allowed him to develop his talents to the full.

Lieber was born in Berlin on March 18, 1800 as the tenth of 13 children. As a boy he had been influenced by Jahn and his ideals. He fought against Napoleon at Belle Allianee and at Namur where he was severely wounded and barely survived — he was just about 15. Because of his love of freedom, he was expelled from Berlin University and ended up in prison. After some difficulties, he succeeded in obtaining his degree from Jena and then joined the Greek rebellion against the Turks. In 1822, he escaped to Italy. Hungry and without a penny, he made his way to Rome where he found a patron in the Prussian ambassador Niebuhr who, however, was not able to obtain permission for him to return to Berlin. Niebuhr counseled him to emigrate to America.

During a year in London, he saved the money for the passage by teaching German and Italian. On June 20, 1827, Lieber arrived in New York and immediately went to Boston where he was most warmly received by men so prominent as Josiah Quincy, President of Harvard University, and the historians Preston and Bancroft, the latter a great friend of Germany and later ambassador in Berlin.

Following the pattern of the seventh edition of the Brockhaus' "Konversationslexikon" he edited the first edition of the Encyclopedia Americana for the publishing house of Cary in Philadelphia and wrote a number of articles himself in perfect English.

On September 21, 1829, Lieber married Mathilda Oppenheimer, who had followed him from England. In 1834 he became professor of Girard College in Philadelphia and in 1835 he was appointed professor of history and political science at the College — today University — of South Carolina. He remained there until 1856. An unyielding abolitionist, only his personal popularity allowed him to remain there so long. From 1856 onward, Lieber was a professor at New York's Columbia University. In the Civil War he was commissioned by President Lincoln to write the "Code of War and Government for the Armies for the United States on the Field" which was published by the War Department as General Order 100. It was the first modern codification of martial law.

Lieber continued to receive honorary assignments from the government until his death in New York on October 2, 1872.

Ernst Lubitsch

The "Lubitsch-touch" was a trademark even beyond the world of film. Josef von Sternberg, not precisely a friend of Lubitsch, defined the Lubitsch touch as "the basic idea . . . that someone, regardless of what happened, kept an amused twinkle in his eye and never lost his cool." Lubitsch, a Berliner (born in 1892), whose father tried to dissuade him from a theatrical career, attracted attention at a very early age appearing in comic and grotesque roles, including that of the Hunchback in "Sumurun" under the direction of Max Reinhardt. Lubitsch later made a film of "Sumurun."

He went into the motion picture industry, a field then regarded with social disapproval. He became a director and was soon very successful with comedies, such as "Kohlhiesel's Daughters."

Lubitsch's major creative period began after World War I. With films such as "Madame Dubarry" (1919) and "Anne Boleyn" (1920), now considered classics, he became a "humanizer of history." His leading actors were Pola Negri and Emil Jannings. Although filmed in impoverished postwar Berlin, these films could compete even on a technical level with expensive Hollywood productions.

He began to attract attention in America and after the successful run of his film "Madame Dubarry," called "one of the most outstanding films of our time" by the New York Times, he went to Hollywood.

Lubitsch became famous after directing Mary Pickford in "Rosita" in 1923. His next picture, the stylish comedy "The Marriage Circle" (1924), also was a box-office success. Film after film revealed his unique cinematographic imagination: "Forbidden Paradise" (1924), "Kiss Me Again" (1925), "Lady Windermere's Fan" (1925), "So this is Paris" (1926). In all these films he developed "this disdainful twinkle of continental wit." With the advent of sound, he also explored new recording techniques in such films as "The Love Parade" (1929) and "Monte Carlo" (1930) with Maurice Chevalier and Jeanette MacDonald.

One of Lubitsch's greatest successes was "Ninotchka," (1939) in which Greta Garbo played the lead and which starred such famous Berlin actors as Granach, Bressart and Lorre. "This film by Lubitsch," the New York Times stated, "is worth at least a thousand words more than we can print here."

Many other famous films were to follow, such as "The Shop around the Corner," "To Be or Not to Be," and "Heaven can Wait." In addition to his activities as a director, Lubitsch also became a producer during the 40's.

Lubitsch died suddenly in 1947. "We shall never again see men like him," stated an obituary. "The world they celebrated has perished," it said. "Even before he himself died, it lived on only in Lubitsch's memory."

Ottmar Mergenthaler

Ottmar Mergenthaler, from Hachtel in Baden-Wuerttemberg's Tauber valley, has been called a second Gutenberg. Like Gutenberg, Mergenthaler revolutionized the art of printing. Prior to Mergenthaler's invention of the linotype, no newspaper in the world had more than eight pages.

Born May 11, 1854, Mergenthaler was the son of a poor village school teacher who moved soon after Ottmar's birth to Ensingen, on the Enz river. There the clock in the church's bell tower had stood still for years, and no clockmaker had been able to repair it. One evening, however, the bells suddenly rang at evensong. "The schoolmaster's boy has done it!" was the surprised reaction.

Mergenthaler's ambition at that time was to become a watchmaker. Although his father was initially opposed to the idea, after some hesitation he apprenticed him to a relative named Hahl in Bietigheim, where he soon earned a journeyman's wage.

"Here," he later recalled, "I learned precision and recognized that one has to look at the mechanism as a whole if a watch is to function."

One day he admitted to his master that he wanted to go to America. Again there were problems with his family and also with Hahl. In the end, Hahl's son in Washington paid for his passage. On October 26, 1872, the "Berlin" docked in Baltimore, bringing 500 passengers in steerage. Among them was a slender, handsome young man of medium height with blue eyes and red-blond hair, carrying only a wooden suitcase carved by peasants from his neighborhood.

At first, Mergenthaler worked on knives and tools in August Hahl's shop, and obtained his first patent at the age of 20. As business was rather poor, Hahl moved to Baltimore where Mergenthaler became a member of the Liederkranz Society and of the German Turnverein. He always had more ideas than time to execute them. Word of his talents soon spread.

On August 17, 1876, a stranger, Charles Moore, entered the shop, of which Mergenthaler had become co-owner. Moore told him he held a patent on a typewriter for newspapers which was designed to eliminate type-setting by hand, but that it just did not work. He asked Mergenthaler whether he could construct a better model.

Mergenthaler promptly recognized that Moore's design was faulty, but set about improving it. Two years later, he had assembled a machine that stamped letters and words on cardboard. But that was not what he had envisioned.

He then worked like a man possessed to construct what was to capture the attention of the world under the name of "Linotype." In doing so, he had to overcome many difficulties. One night, fire destroyed the shop, including all his designs and models. He knew, however, that if he succeeded, his invention would mean "more books—more education for all. At home we had no money for school books..."

He found a supporter in Whitelaw Reid of the New York Tribune. Finally, while riding on a train, the idea came to him: why a separate machine for casting and another for stamping? Why not stamp the letters and immediately cast them in metal in the same machine?

Much effort and another fifty patents were required before he could show a more or less usable model to the New York Tribune on July 3, 1886. There followed fights with shareholders and unions. And the press even in Germany attacked him vehemently. Finally success came with many honors, including a trip to his old home town.

Soon afterwards, Mergenthaler contracted tuberculosis. He nonetheless continued to work unceasingly until his death at the early age of 44 in Baltimore on October 28,1899.

Christian Metz

Christian Metz (born in Neuwied on December 30, 1794), spent his childhood in Ronneburg in Hesse, and was the founder of the Amana

OTTMAR MERGENTHALER

Colonies, seven villages near the mouth of the Iowa River that are best known today for the quality of household appliances and many other products manufactured there.

In Amana, where church services are still conducted in German and where many of the 2000 residents still speak the language of their ancestors, the name of Christian Metz still evokes reverence. Metz was the intellectual and spiritual leader of this religious group that emigrated to New York in 1842 and subsequently to Iowa in order to escape religious persecution.

Amana was a communal religious experiment that was able to realize its utopia to a considerable extent. Industriousness, a sense of community, piety, and skill as artisans soon gained respect for the people of Amana and enabled them to distribute their products widely. Under the leadership of Metz, the colony achieved greater prosperity and internal harmony than any other utopian settlement. Metz died on July 27, 1867, and the flourishing community remained a communal system until 1932, having endured longer than any comparable experiment.

In response to the depression of 1932, the people of Amana agreed to a thorough reorganization under which the church and the colony were administered separately and private property was introduced. A joint-stock corporation was formed to administer the secular holdings of the community, and the communal kitchen was disbanded. Amana once again prospered and continues to do so. The name of Christian Metz is still remembered in Amana with love and gratitude.

John O. Meusebach

John O. Meusebach, the founder of Fredericksburg in Texas, was born in Dillenburg in Hesse-Nassau on May 26, 1812 and grew up in Baumgartenbrueck near Potsdam. In 1845, he was given the thankless task of salvaging as much as possible from the failure of the German colonization in eastern Texas. The verdict of history: the former student proved himself a master.

In 1843, the Association of Mainz Nobility chartered a company for German settlements in eastern Texas, appointing Carl Friedrich Prince of Solms-Braunfels as its Commissioner General. Solms founded New Braunfels, but the lands that the Mainz immigrants thought they had bought either did not exist or were in Indian

territory. The situation of the settlers became more and more misera-
ble, especially when the promised supplies from Mainz failed to
arrive and thousands of colonists were lost.

At that point, Count Castel, the Chairman of the Mainz Association, approached Baron Hans Otfried von Meusebach. Meusebach,
who had grown up in a liberal atmosphere and been influenced as a
young man by Sealsfield's views concerning America, had long
considered the idea of emigrating to the new continent. The enthusiastic songs about Texas by the poet, Hoffman von Fallersleben,
which were then a kind of underground literature in Germany, also
influenced his decision. Meusebach sailed for Texas to look for
Solms, to whom he was to present his credentials. The Prince had
already started the trip home. By coincidence, Meusebach encountered him in the port of Galveston just in time to pay Solms' debts.

Meusebach led the colonists further into the interior. He was
able to reach an agreement with the Indians, founded Fredericksburg
and finally, after initial difficulties, established an orderly community. He then proceeded to found the colonies of Castel and Leiningen
in Llano county.

In 1851, Meusebach was elected State Senator for Comal, Bexar
and Medina Counties. In that same year he returned for a brief period
to Berlin. He spent the greater part of his life in Fredericksburg,
which honored him on its 50th anniversary. He died on May 27,
1897, at age 85.

The Muhlenberg Family

Muhlenberg College in Allentown, Pennsylvania, was named in
honor of a family that played an extraordinary role in American
history. On November 25, 1742, Pastor Heinrich Melchior
Muehlenberg (born in Einbeck on September 6, 1711) arrived in
Philadelphia from the town of Halle for the purpose of organizing the
Lutheran Church. His congregation extended from New York to
Georgia. He founded churches in Providence, Pa., and Philadelphia,
and organized the first Lutheran Synod on August 14, 1748.

Muhlenberg also initiated close ties between America and the
University of Goettingen, which Benjamin Franklin had visited in
1765. Although his early advocacy of American independence
created many difficulties for him, he was proud that his sons helped

fight for America's independence. He died on October 7, 1787, in Trappe (New Providence, Pa.).

His oldest son, John Peter Gabriel (October 1, 1746–October 1, 1807) planned to become a pastor and returned to Halle to study theology. After a brief period of study, he joined an English regiment of Dragoniers being dispatched to America, ostensibly in order to secure his free return passage. A friend of his father assisted him in getting out of the English army immediately upon his return to Philadelphia on January 15, 1767. In 1768, he was ordained and appointed assistant pastor at the Zions and St. Pauls Church in New Jersey, whose membership spoke German. Shortly thereafter, he was asked to serve as minister to the Swedish-German congregations in Virginia. Here, "it was due to Muhlenberg and a few others that the Germans did not stand aside in those long months in which the spirit of freedom took root in Virginia." He was subsequently always in the forefront of the anti-colonialist movement. He was the leader of a great protest assembly that met on June 16, 1774, and on January 10,1775, he served as president of a newly founded defense committee.

When hostilities broke out, Muhlenberg assumed the task of forming a regiment of Germans from Virginia. His farewell sermon in Woodstock, where a large congregation of mountain people had assembled to bid their beloved pastor farewell, ended with the words, "Everything has its season, a time to preach and a time to fight—and that has come now." Muhlenberg then took off his clerical robes and stepped down from the pulpit in the uniform he had worn underneath.

George Washington had respect for Muhlenberg's German regiment, which took part in many battles. The German soldiers from Virginia even occasionally had to fight against German troops under British command. In early 1783, Muhlenberg was named Major General. He did not return to the clergy after the war. He settled in Philadelphia and went into public life, first as Deputy Chairman of the Pennsylvania State Council, then as a congressman for several terms and later as senator from Pennsylvania. After that, President Jefferson had other assignments for him. Muhlenberg was active in the German Society of Pennsylvania (founded in 1774) whose purpose was to aid poor and exploited German immigrants. He died in Philadelphia.

His younger brother, Frederick Augustus Conrad also played an important role in the emergence of the United States. He, too, studied theology in Halle and was ordained in Reading, Pennsylvania, on

31

MAJOR GENERAL PETER MUHLENBERG

March 2, 1779. He was elected to the Continental Congress on March 2, 1779. Friedrich August Muhlenberg subsequently served as first Speaker of the House of Congress from 1789 to 1791, and again held the post of Speaker from 1793 to 1795.

Friedrich Münch

Friedrich Muench, pastor, student leader, humanist, prairie farmer, state senator in Missouri, poet and wine connoisseur, one of the most sympathetic figures of the liberal emigration of 1833, was one of the group of state founders. The son of a pastor, he was born in Niedergemuenden in Hesse on June 25, 1799. Together with the Follen brothers Karl, Ludwig and Paul, he organized the Giessen Black Fraternity. Like so many others, they were disappointed by the Metternich reaction that set in after the wars of liberation against Napoleon. Their writings, which were strongly influenced by the circle of the "Young Germany" authors, share some similarities with those of the German "Wandervogel" youth movement prior to World War I.

After the Hambach Festival of 1832, when police pressure became more intensive, Muench and Paul Follen (the other Follen brothers had already left), decided to initiate mass emigration to North America. For this purpose, they founded the Giessen Emigration Society in 1833. Their goal was to establish states within the United States, which were to be German in every respect and only loosely tied to the federal government in Washington. They hoped such states might be used to prepare the revolution in Germany, and thus to achieve its unification.

Muench and Follen each led a group of emigrants to the U.S. Hardly had they arrived than they realized that their idea was a mirage, and the group disbanded. Muench and Follen settled in Warren County in the 12-year-old state of Missouri. Muench wrote in his memoirs that "it was impractical to create a kind of ready free state in Germany which one could simply transplant to America without much ado. Quick mass settlement is impossible. But the need for German settlements is still present, just that things must be done quietly and carefully.''

Muench and Follen adjusted to American reality and were content. Follen died young. Muench was active in German-American organizations, and founded aid organizations for the large number of refugees from the 1848/49 uprisings. The "Grey" ones of 1833 at first found it difficult to get along with them.

Muench later played an historic role while serving as a senator in the state of Missouri. Largely as a result of his popularity and rhetorical skills, Missouri did not intervene in the Civil War on the side of the South, a fact which considerably improved the situation of the North.

A visible sign of his popularity was that his colleagues in the Senate permitted Muench, as a single exception, to smoke his pipe during sessions. ''Papa Muench,'' as he was known everywhere, was especially proud of his vineyards. The following is a stanza from his Catawba Song that was popular with German-Americans:

O you brothers far on the Rhine
if only you were here with us
if you, too, drank Missouri wine
if you were free, free like us.

Friedrich Muench died at age 82 while pruning his beloved vineyards.

Thomas Nast

Christmas Eve, 1869, was the beginning of the end of Boss Tweed and his companions, who for years had robbed the city of New York in the most brazen manner. They were done in by a cartoon in Harper's Weekly by Thomas Nast. Nast, as the father of American political cartoonists, was the nemesis of this gang of criminals. On the basis of one of Nast's drawings, Boss Tweed, who had fled to Italy, was recognized, arrested, and extradited.

Other familiar symbols created by Nast are the donkey of the Democrats and the elephant of the Republicans. In adopting their respective party emblems, neither Democrats nor Republicans seem to have realized that both donkey and elephant were expressions of Nast's biting irony.

Nast portrayed New York's Tammany Hall, the institution he fought for decades, as a tiger baring its teeth.

Nast was no weathervane. Born in Landau on September 27, 1840, the son of liberal parents, he grew up sharing the ideals that preceded the 1848 revolution. His father, a trumpeter in a military band, emigrated to New York in 1846. The son, who had a passion for drawing, worked successfully, starting at age 14 for the magazines of Frank Leslie, who was then very influential. Leslie sent him to cover a world boxing championship in London in 1860. Unfortunately, he sent no fees, so Nast proceeded to Italy, where he witnessed Garibaldi's struggle for freedom. Nast first encountered war in Italy.

Upon returning to New York, Harper's Weekly sent him to Washington to cover Lincoln's inauguration. Nast reported, "I felt as if the shadow of death was everywhere — I felt war approaching. I tried to work in my hotel room but could not do it, . . . my heart was heavy."

Thomas Nast became a chronicler of the Civil War, loyally devoted to the cause of the Union and to the freeing of the slaves. Shortly before his own death, Lincoln said that "our cause had no better campaigner than Thomas Nast — his allegorical drawings never failed to rouse deep enthusiasm and they always came when we needed them most."

During the Civil War Nast created today's image of Santa Claus, recalling Knecht Ruprecht from his youth in Germany. Since he was his own model, his Santa Claus is rather small, heavy, and smiling somewhat shrewdly. The Union soldiers, for whom he had drawn "Santa Claus in Camp" and "Christmas Eve," sent him hundreds of letters of appreciation. Year after year, Nast's public clamored for his Santa Claus drawings, and in 1889, Harper's issued a volume of "Thomas Nast's Christmas Drawings for the Human Race."

Nast untiringly used his pencil to fight corruption, exploitation, and government abuses, and to aid exploited minorities, including Negroes, Indians and Chinese. President Grant became his friend and wrote, "Two things helped me most to win the election, Sheridan's sword and Thomas Nast's pencil." Grant's friendship, however, proved expensive to Nast, who invested his entire fortune in the publishing company founded by Grant after he left office for the purpose of publishing his memoirs. Nast and Grant lost everything.

ANNA OTTENDORFER

Nast was poor, bitter and virtually forgotten when President Theodore Roosevelt remembered him. Roosevelt recalled his indebtedness to Nast in his observation, ''I owe my first lesson in practical politics to Thomas Nast.'' Roosevelt appointed Nast consul to Ecuador. Nast died there of yellow fever on December 7, 1902.

Anna Ottendorfer

Anna Ottendorfer (February 13, 1815–April 1, 1884), a philanthropist, founded the Isabella Nursing Home in New York, which even today is considered exemplary. This act alone would have sufficed to secure her a place of honor in the ''Year of the Woman.'' In addition to being very generous, she was a self-made woman of admirable strength of character when women had difficulty finding a place within the economy.

Her father was the businessman Eduard Behr, from Wuerzburg. He was unable to give what his daughter so urgently wanted, university training. As that was not yet available, she resolved in 1836, despite parental protest, to emigrate to America, where an older brother lived on a farm in Niagara County. She did not, however, remain for long on the farm. She made the acquaintance of a young printer, Jacob Uhl, married him and moved to New York. Uhl was employed by the New York Staatszeitung, which at that time was a small weekly produced at a book-printing plant. By economizing, the young couple was able, a few years later, to purchase on installment half of the printing plant from Julius Boettcher, with a down payment of $72. Soon thereafter, the Uhls took over the whole printing and production operation of the Staatszeitung, and gradually they made this German-language paper, which had become a daily, into one of the best in America. Anna was editor, secretary, assisted at typesetting, and also distributed the papers when necessary.

When Uhl died on April 25, 1852, Anna rejected all offers from prospective purchasers of the publishing operation. In 1859, she married her collaborator, Oswald Ottendorfer, and under their direction both the paper and the publishing operation grew. Anna remained active in the business, but she also began to direct her enormous energy to helping suffering people. In 1875, she founded a nursing home for women in Astoria which was later transferred to the Bronx. The home was named for her daughter, Isabella, who died in 1873.

She then founded the Hermann Uhl Memorial Fund in honor of her son, Hermann, who died in 1881. The purpose of the Fund was to aid German schools and teacher seminars in America.

Anna Ottendorfer made a large donation to the German Dispensary, which is now Lenox Hill Hospital, enabling the construction of the Ottendorfer Pavilion. She provided land for the German Dispensary from her own funds, endowed the German Hospital in Newark, and contributed large sums when the areas near the Rhine and Weichsel were damaged by floods in Germany in 1882. She did so without any publicity. Her husband, who managed the editorial affairs of the Staatszeitung, remained in the background of her philanthropic activities but made large donations himself after her death. These included an endowment of an important library of German topics at the University of the State of New York. The Ottendorfer branch of the New York Public Library is named after him.

Erwin Panofsky

The art historian, Erwin Panofsky (born in Hannover on March 30, 1892, died in Princeton, New Jersey, on March 14, 1968) became a mentor to an entire generation of scholars in America. His influence extended into many areas, especially literature and music. In his obituary, Herbert von Einem stated, ''Wherever in the last decades problems of scholarship or methodology in art history were discussed or where intellectual and historical contexts and traditions were being documented, Panofsky's work was referred to as an indispensable foundation in all nations that took an interest in such questions.

Panofsky's readable style and his ability to explain complicated problems in an easily understandable format helped him attain an unprecedented measure of influence as an art historian. His books, some of them in paperback, were printed in large editions. If the statement is true that German scholars after 1933 made art history and musical scholarship ''ripe for college,'' it is mainly the result of Panofsky's work. He selflessly assisted other prominent German scholars in receiving appointments at the internationally famous Institute for Advanced Studies in Princeton.

Von Einem wrote of Panofsky that ''despite all obstacles, the years of his work in Germany brought rich, more than rich, fruit,'' stressing that ''there is no visible break between Panofsky's work in

Germany and that in America, except for the language.''

Panofsky grew up in Berlin, where he attended the Joachims-thaler High School, which concentrated on ancient languages and history. He often expressed his gratitude to the school, to which he owed his broad humanistic education and his mastery of ancient languages. In 1915, he gained sudden fame in the art world with his work on ''Duerer's Theory of Art.'' In collaboration with Fritz Saxl, he published a book on ''Duerer's Melancolia I'' in 1923, which also attracted much attention. Panofsky always affirmed his indebtedness to Aby Warburg, the collector and art critic in whose Hamburg Library he worked for many years. Following Warburg's lead, he stressed throughout his work the idea of the methodological unity and methodological union of all areas and all directions in the history of ideas.

Panofsky taught at Hamburg University from 1926–1933, and was in New York as a guest lecturer when he learned of his dismissal in 1933. He decided to remain here, and in 1935 was appointed to Princeton, where he soon became Dean of the Institute for Advanced Studies. He wrote books in rapid succession, the most famous of which is possibly ''Studies in Iconology,'' which was published in 1939. The term ''iconology'' is now inseparably identified with Panofsky's name. While ''iconography'' describes and classifies attributes of persons, ideas or institutions, ''iconology'' explores their significance within the framework of human and cultural history and emphasizes synthesis rather than analysis. Panofsky's entire work represents a synthesis of German preoccupation with ideas and American scholarship. Panofsky was a humanist with a keen sense of humor, love for his fellowman and an understanding of the art of knowing how to live. In 1967, the Federal Republic of Germany awarded him the order of ''Pour le Mérite.''

Franz Daniel Pastorius

Dr. Franz Daniel Pastorius, born in Sommerhausen in Franconia on September 26, 1651, is a name that marks the beginning of German immigration to North America. He was the leader of the 13 families from Krefeld who, at the urging of the Quaker leader, William Penn, landed in Philadelphia on October 6, 1683. Philadelphia at that time had only two streets.

The ship on which these first German settlers arrived, the "Concord," has been called the German "Mayflower." Pastorius founded Germantown, now a part of Philadelphia, which became the center for Germans who, like Pastorius, had been persecuted in their homeland because of their religion. The first German settlers were Pietists, who soon became Quakers in America.

Pastorius was a lawyer, mayor and teacher, and founded the first evening school for adults. He was also a poet, the first in the New World. He became a friend of Penn's and an untiring helper of new immigrants. To him we owe our precise records of the first German settlement: "We called the place Germantown (in English). Some gave it the name Poor-town. It may neither be described nor believed by posterity under what conditions of need and poverty but with what Christian serenity and untiring industry this German township was founded..."

He described the town seal to his father as "a grapevine, a sprig of flax and a weaver's spool with the inscription 'vinum, linum et textrinum' to show that here people earn their living honorably and under God through growing grapes and flax, and through workmanship." On November 16, 1684, Pastorius organized the first fair in Philadelphia which became the model for the American country fair. Earnings were small, "because the newcomers from Germany and England usually bring so much clothing with them that they need no more for several years..." This situation soon changed, and cloth from Germantown was sold to New York and Boston.

On February 18, 1688, Pastorius and three of his fellow citizens made the first protest against Negro slavery, even though they knew some of their Quaker friends owned slaves. From that time on, slave-holding was not allowed in any of the German religious colonies, even in the South, and was also forbidden in most other German settlements. In 1771, this protest was reflected in Pennsylvania law prohibiting the import of Negroes and Indians into the colony. The London Parliament, however, declared this law void.,

Pastorius' work, "Beehive," is a kind of encyclopedia in Latin, German, English and Dutch, full of good advice and humor. His poem, "Salve Posteritas," addressed to posterity, reveals his ties to the home of his fathers. In the version by the Quaker poet Whittier, under the title "The Pennsylvania Pilgrim," it became one of the classics of American writing.

Pastorius was held in high esteem by all the citizens of Germantown when he died in 1719.

The Roeblings

The Brooklyn Bridge has been called the eighth wonder of the world. ''It opened up the future,'' as someone observed. Johann Augustus Roebling, born in Muehlhausen on June 12, 1806, designed the plans and began construction on the bridge, but did not live to see its completion.

According to family lore, Roebling was one of Hegel's favorite students, and his desire to emigrate to America was strengthened by the philosopher. His friend, Hans Etzler, had been imprisoned for his liberal ideas and had gone to America upon his release. Roebling shared Etzler's ideas, initially even his plan of founding German utopian colonies in America.

Roebling settled in Germania, Pa., later Saxonburg, as a ''Latin Farmer,'' a term applied to German intellectuals who took up farming although they knew more about Cicero than about plowing. He married Johanna Hertig, the daughter of another German immigrant. Roebling had little success as a farmer.

He described his emigration in his ''Diary of my Journey from Muehlhausen in Thuringia via Bremen to the United States in the Year 1831, Written for My Friends.''

Roebling became interested in bridge building. He often recalled the small suspension bridge spanning the river Regnitz in Bamberg and the intense discussions on modern methods of bridge construction with his professor in Berlin; he knew that what he had seen in Europe was only a tentative beginning.

Roebling replaced the chain cables previously used to hold up bridges with a system of wire-rope cables, which were stronger than chain cables. After 1840, he manufactured these wire ropes in his own shop in Saxonburg. Using this new system, he first built the railroad bridge across the Allegheny, then constructed the suspension bridge across the Monongahela near Pittsburgh. In 1851, he offered to link both banks of the Niagara just below the famous falls by means of a suspension bridge. Many people throughout the world, not only in America, considered him a dreamer or even a charlatan. In 1855, the bridge was nonetheless completed. After the long interruption in construction caused by the Civil War, he completed a suspension bridge across the Ohio near Cincinnati in 1867.

He was then ready to realize his dream project of linking Manhattan and Brooklyn. Roebling had to overcome both extraordinary difficulties and many intrigues before starting the preliminary work in 1869. A falling beam squashed his foot, which had to be amputated. Tetanus set in, and he died on July 22, 1869.

His oldest son, Colonel Washington A. Roebling, who had served in the Civil War under General McDowell, completed the bridge after 13 years of hard work, severe accidents and illness. President Chester Alan Arthur and 50,000 visitors from all over the world were present at the opening of the bridge on May 24, 1883.

As Alan Trachtenberg writes in his book on the Brooklyn Bridge, the bridge is both a symbol of American culture and an image of German liberal idealism transplanted to the new world. In the introduction to the book, Stewart Udall, Secretary of the Interior under President Kennedy, observes that the bridge is an object of world history, an inspiration to artists, a monument of industrial culture, a source of inventiveness for engineers, and an awe-inspiring object of beauty for the layman. "His vision was prophetic." The Brooklyn Bridge remains a favorite subject for praise and portrayal.

Ludwig Mies van der Rohe

Ludwig Mies, who joined his name with that of his mother, van der Rohe, was one of the most influential architects of the twentieth century. He often stressed that he wanted to be good rather than original, and observed, "Architecture has nothing to do with the invention of forms, it is no playground for young and old children." His design for a high-rise building near Friedrichstrasse Station in Berlin became the emblem for an entire generation.

Born in Aachen on March 27, 1886, he learned to respect craftsmanship from his father, a stone mason. Like his Bauhaus colleague and friend Walter Gropius, he never passed an academic exam. He was a student of Peter Behrens in Berlin. As a private in World War I, he built bridges and roads in the Balkans and after the war created designs such as that for the Glass House (1921), which elicited both enthusiasm and protest. As Gropius' successor at the Bauhaus in Dessau after 1930, he met the head of the architectural section of New York's Museum of Modern Art, Philip Johnson, who was to become Mies' enthusiastic protagonist in America. Upon

Johnson's suggestion, he became head of the Armour Institute (now Illinois Institute of Technology) in Chicago in 1937. Mies initially had to overcome a number of difficulties, but he was soon known as "the King." "Who better than this poet of steel and glass could have continued the tradition of Chicago's skyscrapers?" queried James Marston Fitch. The Illinois Institute, and its campus built by Mies, had become internationally known by the time of Mies' resignation from the Institute in 1958.

The immense influence of Mies and other architects, who either were German or had grown up in Germany, prompted Henry Luce, publisher of Time and Life, to state that "the revolution in the architecture of the 20th century has been completed, and was completed primarily in America." Luce's observation recalls Benjamin Franklin's comment that "America cultivates best what Germany brought forth . . ." President Kennedy chose Mies as the first person to be awarded the U.S. Medal of Freedom.

Many of Mies' American buildings pointed toward new directions in architecture. Although Mies never abandoned his basic principles, he did depart from the rigorous functionalism of his early period through the use of colored glass, bronze sidings and patios. The Seagram's Building on New York's Park Avenue, designed in collaboration with Johnson, and the Lake Shore Apartments in Chicago, are especially famous. But Mies' influence was not restricted to architecture. He made an impact in many areas, especially in the design of furniture. A chair designed by Mies for the World's Fair in Barcelona, in August 1929, was to become an international model for design after World War II. Mies died on August 17, 1969.

Johann Paul Schott

One can become an American, as George Washington stated, either by birth or by choice. The observation is especially applicable to Johann Paul Schott, former Premier Lieutenant to Frederick the Great of Prussia, who came to New York on his own initiative in early 1776 at the age of 22. He had been educated at the Military Academy in Berlin and was the scion of a wealthy family. Schott arrived with Dutch and British letters of recommendation to Governor Tryon and immediately received an offer to join the English army.

MIES VAN DER ROHE

What he originally had in mind when he sailed from Rotterdam can no longer by ascertained today. Schott left no memoirs, even though much of his life resembles an adventure novel. He never sought the limelight.

What he saw and heard in New York helped him decide to serve the cause of American independence. He had been well received in New York's aristocratic circles, even though he was a commoner. He proceeded, however, to Philadelphia. He easily recognized that the Americans suffered from an extreme shortage of weapons, especially heavy guns and ammunition. He chartered a ship at his own expense and sailed to St. Eustace in the Antilles, where the Dutch maintained a lucrative store of arms for blockade-runners.

Schott purchased weapons and set a course for the coast of Virginia. At the mouth of Chesapeake Bay, he encountered an English fleet. He quickly raised the British flag and dressed his men in British naval uniforms he had stored on board, a maneuver fairly common at that time. He escaped the British, only to be fired upon by American batteries. After another change of flags, he landed in the port of Norfolk with tattered sails.

The War Council wrote Schott a letter of appreciation and asked him to apply for an officer's commission, which he did on September 5, 1776. The following day, he was appointed a major and ordered to New York, which Washington had just entered. Although Governor Tryon and the English Tories had fled to Long Island, Washington was in a precarious position, having only few and badly trained men, and the Battery at the southern tip of Manhattan was under fire from Governor's Island. Schott, not having been attached yet to a specific unit, was waiting to present himself to Washington. He spotted an unused cannon, called some soldiers together on his own authority, had them load the cannon, and scored a perfect hit. Washington thus noticed the young officer and sent him to Colonel Knox, the commander of his artillery. At the Battle of White Plains, Schott was able to demonstrate what he had learned in Prussia.

Washington had to withdraw his decimated army to Pennsylvania. On July 31, 1777, Schott was commissioned to recruit an independent troop of German dragoons and was given permission to use the German language with them. Schott's Dragoons soon became famous. In the battle of Short Hills, he was assigned to cover the withdrawal, was severely wounded, and captured by the British. American prisoners, including Schott, were treated quite brutally at that time. Schott was offered an opportunity to go over to the British side, but he refused, as he later wrote to his friend Richard Rush, the U.S. Attorney General, because ''I had chosen America as my fatherland.''

After six bitter months from which he was not to recover for a long time, Schott was exchanged along with some other prisoners. He resumed command over his dragoons and, although he remained sickly, fought in several battles before being named commander of Fort Wyoming in Pennsylvania.

After the end of the war, Schott, like many other former German officers such as Steuben and Lutterloh, remained in America. He made his home in Wilkes-Barre, was elected to the Pennsylvania House of Deputies, and became one of the most active champions of unification of the former colonies. But his career as a fighter had not yet come to an end. In May, 1788, he again recruited a troop of dragoons to intervene in insurgencies and once again his troops were German.

In 1791, Schott was elected judge of Lucerne County, an office which he held until 1804. He was given a high post in the fiscal administration in Pennsylvania. He died at the age of 85.

Carl Schurz

Carl Schurz, in the words of Edward Channing, was ''the greatest German of their immigration.'' On the occasion of Schurz's 100th birthday, the German Foreign Minister, Gustav Stresemann, said that ''Schurz forged love of Germany and loyalty to his American fatherland into the wonderful integrity of a great personality.''

Schurz fled Germany as a revolutionary of 1848, because he wanted to see his homeland free from division and united into a democracy. In America, he found ''the bulwark and the home of liberty,'' but never denied his German heritage. An orator, following the model of Cicero, he mastered the subtleties of the English language and spoke without an accent. He continued to speak German with his family and among German friends. As an American, he evaluated the situation in Germany from the perspective of American democracy, but he measured American conditions against his youthful dream of liberty. He steadily fought to make these dreams come true, unafraid of and undefeated by a multitude of obstacles. His Rhineland humor helped him to overcome many disappointments.

The moral imperatives that had motivated him in Germany made him a champion of the abolition movement in America. "From his knightly youth onward he remained a servant and champion of truth," as the poet R. W. Gilder wrote after his death.

Born in the tenant quarters of Gracht Castle in Liblar near Bonn, Schurz wanted to become a historian. Under the guidance of his teacher, Professor Gottfried Kinkel, he joined the liberal wing of the student movement. During the May uprising of 1849, he was an officer of the defenders of the fortress of Rastatt in Baden, which was then under siege by Prussian regulars. He knew that death by firing squad or hanging awaited him after surrender had been agreed upon. While on patrol, Schurz, a keen observer, discovered an unfinished sewage tunnel that led out of the fortress and to freedom, and he escaped through this channel with his batman and another comrade.

He fled to Switzerland, where he earned a meager living through teaching. His mentor, Kinkel, who had also become his friend, had been taken captive and condemned by a military tribunal to life imprisonment in a fortress. But the Prussian King arbitrarily changed this sentence, which was still considered honorable, to common imprisonment. The decision provoked a general outcry. Disguised and equipped with the passport of a relative, Schurz returned to Germany and freed Kinkel from the Spandau penitentiary near Berlin. They escaped to England via Rostock, and Schurz became famous for his daring rescue of Kinkel.

In London, Schurz met the sister of another German refugee, Margarethe Meyer from Hamburg, whom he married on July 6, 1852.

"The fatherland was closed to me," he wrote later. "England was alien to me and would always remain so. Where to go? America, I told myself . . . Ubi libertas, ibi patria."

He sailed for America in August of 1852. The first way station was Philadelphia, where he lived with his family until 1855. A year later, he acquired a farm in Watertown, Wisconsin, and at the same time adopted the cause of abolition as his own. Even before becoming a citizen, he was nominated as Lieutenant Governor, but the voters rejected him. His first major political battle was against the xenophobic party of the Know-Nothings. Through a speech in April, 1859, about the "true Americans," he helped defeat them and became a widely acclaimed speaker.

He practiced law in Milwaukee after 1858, and joined the young Republican Party, which was in opposition to the slave-holding

CARL SCHURZ

plantation owners of the South. During the campaign trip, Schurz met Lincoln, who wrote him shortly afterward on July 18, 1860, that "within the limits of our brief acquaintance I may tell you that no man is closer to my heart than you are."

After the outbreak of the Civil War, President Lincoln appointed Schurz Minister to Spain. Schurz had asked permission to form a cavalry regiment of Germans in New York, but Lincoln considered his presence in Spain considerably more important. There was a danger that Madrid and several other European countries might recognize the Confederacy of the secessionist Southern states, an eventuality that Lincoln had to prevent at any price. At that time, the Northern states had not yet much success militarily. Most Europeans were disappointed that Lincoln had not immediately proclaimed the freedom of the slaves. Schurz felt that if he had done so, Lincoln would have had public opinion on his side. Schurz had obtained the right to communicate directly with the President and expressed his opinion openly. Lincoln hesitated. He was primarily interested in ending the Civil War and in reuniting the North and the South.

Schurz asked to be recalled and to be given a field command. In the White House he made no secret of his conviction in favor of abolition. Nobody had spoken so frankly to the President before who, despite his principal interest, was at first opposed. But after some hesitation, he followed the advice of his loyal counselor. Schurz was appointed Major General and given command over a division formed mostly of German immigrants, who fought near Chancellorsville and Gettysburg with varying success. Schurz was then attacked by jealous rivals. Military historians have subsequently completely rehabilitated Schurz as a leader of his troops and proved that his courage was never in doubt. As an officer, too, Schurz showed more than mere physical courage. Once, he received an order under military regulations to execute a young deserter. Convinced that the soldier, still just a boy, had simply lost his nerve, Schurz let the time for the execution pass and sent a request for a pardon to Lincoln. Lincoln agreed, and the soldier later fought bravely.

After Lincoln's assassination, Schurz emphatically advocated a policy of reconciliation with the defeated South. Shortly after his 40th birthday, on March 4, 1869, he entered the U.S. Senate in Washington as Senator for the State of Missouri. From 1877 to 1881 he held the office of Secretary of the Interior under President Hayes.

In this office he laid the foundations to preserve the natural riches of the nation, brought order and dignity to relations with the severely pressed Indian tribes and the American government. He introduced a system of qualifications to the civil service thereby removing lower and middle level civil servants from political influence.

Even before the founding of the German empire, Schurz had traveled back to the old home country, where he had two long talks with Bismarck who confessed to him that "as a German I admire you." Schurz died on May 14, 1906, deeply mourned by a great circle of friends and admirers.

𝕸𝖆𝖗𝖙𝖎𝖓 𝕾𝖈𝖍𝖜𝖆𝖗𝖟𝖘𝖈𝖍𝖎𝖑𝖉

Martin Schwarzschild holds a leading place among American astronomers. He was born in Potsdam on May 31, 1912, His father, Karl Schwarzschild (born in Frankfurt/Main on October 9, 1873; died in Potsdam on May 11, 1916) conducted pioneering experiments in photographic photometry of the stars while director of the Astrophysical Observatory in Potsdam. Observations made by the elder Schwarzschild on problems of the movement of fixed stars provided insights essential to the theory of relativity later developed by Albert Einstein, whom the younger Scharzschild was to meet in Princeton.

When Martin Schwarzschild, who received his doctorate from Göttingen University in 1935, had to emigrate, he first worked at the Institute for Astrophysics in Oslo before coming to America in 1937.

From 1942 until 1945 he served as an officer in the U.S. Army. Since 1947, he has taught Astronomics in Princeton, New Jersey, where, so to speak, he has continued his father's work. Schwarzschild is considered "a driving force in the development of theoretical astronomics in America which until then received less attention than astronomical observations," as Laura Fermi states in her book, "Illustrious Immigrants."

Schwarzschild did not remain content with theoretical computations alone, however. He used stratospheric balloons to carry telescopes to photograph the sun and the fixed stars. In his writings he has made important contributions on the internal structure of the stars. His major work is "Evolution and Structure of the Stars" (1958).

Schwarzschild has made a special study of the high temperature gases which form the solar corona, computing the strength of the waves emanating from the solar surface. Computations contained in his breakthrough discoveries were used to prepare for the lunar landing.

The Academy of Sciences in Göttingen is one of many institutions that have honored him.

Charles Proteus Steinmetz

Charles Proteus Steinmetz, the "Wizard of Schenectady" to whom electrical engineering — and General Electric — owe pioneering inventions, was almost rejected by an immigration official at the Castle Gardens in New York. He was a cripple, small, lame, could show no money and knew hardly a word of English. The clerk could not know that he was a mathematical genius, and if he had it would have hardly interested him. But throughout his life this man, to whom fate had been so unkind, knew how to gain and keep loyal friends. His friend Assmussen, who had sailed to America with him on the steerage deck of the emigrant ship La Champagne, and who had already lived in America before, showed the clerk a large sum of money, claiming that he had only kept it for Steinmetz. Assmussen was tall, strong, and spoke English fluently. After some hesitation, Steinmetz was allowed to go ashore.

Born on April 9, 1865 in Breslau, the son of a printer, Karl Heinrich Steinmetz—who was also a cripple—and his wife Caroline neé Neubert, Karl (he later changed his name to Charles and added the name Proteus—the old sea spirit—that fellow-students had given him) showed an extraordinary interest in mathematics and physics from his earliest days. For many years, even though his parents and his grandmother rather spoiled him, he felt himself to be an outsider because of his misshapen form. But during his student years, he was drawn to the socialist circles in Breslau, at first through a "Mathematics Association." He met Heinrich Lux who, at that time, was full of enthusiasm for utopian settlements in America, as well as the young Gerhard Hauptmann who, in his Breslau years, was also interested in the idea.

When Lux and others were arrested, Steinmetz began to edit the socialist "People's Voice" but in 1888 found it advisable to leave Germany. Via Austria and Zurich, he arrived in New York on July 1, 1889.

Rudolf Eichemeyer, one of the "Forty-Eighters" who had emigrated because of his convictions and now ran a factory in Yonkers that manufactured machines to make hats, sponsored Steinmetz. Eichemeyer, who himself had registered a few patents for inventions of his own, was interested in the electrical engineering industry which, at that time, was still in its infancy. He soon realized the extraordinary talents of his new employee.

Steinmetz had hardly learned English when one of his lectures on hysteresis before the American Institute of Electrical Engineering, attracted great attention (January 19, 1892). During that same year, Steinmetz went to work for General Electric, which soon moved its laboratories to Schenectady. Steinmetz made the move upon the urging of Eichemeyer, who always proved to be a true friend.

His inventions often made the headlines; newspapers called him "a modern Jupiter throwing his lightning bolts." He also worked with Edison. His major inventions involved alternating current, based on complex computations.

Steinmetz always went his own way. His greenhouse, in which he grew unusual plants, was often the subject of — not always friendly — articles. It was said that he preferred ugly, prickly plants.

Steinmetz did not marry. But he "adopted" Joseph Le Roy Hayden, an engineer, and lived happily with his family and was called grandpa by his children.

Several universities awarded him honorary doctoral degrees and at the Union University in Schenectady he held a post as professor of electrical engineering.

Steinmetz did not abandon his socialist ideals, but tried to find a common denominator for them and the American economic system in which he played so prominent a role. To this end, he wrote his book, "America and the New Time," in which he urged a four-hour day. The fact that Germany, to which he was still emotionally attached, was at war against his chosen home, America, affected him profoundly. Since he spoke his mind, he suffered severe attacks, which he disregarded. Even while World War I was going on, he propagated the idea of a united Europe — without, however, receiving much of an echo. Old acquaintances purposely did not see him. But things changed after the end of the war, and he was soon put in charge of the school administration in Schenectady. When Einstein traveled to America on a lecture tour in 1921, he visited Steinmetz and the two got involved in a long discussion on mathematics.

Steinmetz died in his sleep on October 26, 1923.

The Steinway Dynasty

Steinway concert grand pianos are known all over the world, and for more than a century the names of famous virtuosi have been closely associated with the Steinway name. Indeed, the musical life of America and of the world is inconceivable without Steinway, a firm that still remains in the family.

On tours of the White House, visitors are fascinated by the large concert grand in the East Room. It is known as the "golden grand" and is decorated with the insignia of the United States. The 300,000th instrument built by the firm, it is a gift from the house of Steinway. Another Steinway grand, on which President Harry S. Truman frequently played, now stands in the Truman Library in Independence. The Steinways presented the White House with its first piano in 1903, during Theodore Roosevelt's term.

When Theodore E. Steinway presented the "golden grand" to President Franklin Delano Roosevelt on December 10, 1938, he referred to the year 1903: "We are responding to the same motives as then — namely, to give a sign of our gratitude that we, as foreigners on these friendly shores, were permitted to make our home and live our lives here and carry on our work in happiness and contentment..."

The founder of the dynasty, Heinrich Engelhard Steinweg (who changed his name to Henry Engelhard Steinway) was from Wolfshagen, Brunswick. Born February 22, 1797, his childhood and youth were difficult. During the Napoleonic War, several of his brothers were killed, the family house was burned down, and at age 15 he lost his father and his last surviving brother. Although he had no musical training, he early displayed a talent for building musical instruments. The first instrument he made was a zither. In 1818, he started work in an organ builder's shop, learned how to play the organ, and became a church organist. His interest in building instruments increased, but the date he built his first piano in Seesen is not known. Alfred Dolge ("Pianos and their Makers") asserts that he built the first one in February 1825 for his bride, Juliane Thiemer, by whom he had seven children. According to family legend, Steinweg built his first piano in his kitchen. In any event, he was able to display one concert grand and two other pianos at the Braunschweig fair in 1839, for which he was awarded the first prize of a gold medal.

The uprisings of 1848–49 in Germany did not leave the Steinweg family untouched and the family business that had been so arduously built up suffered. One of the sons, Henry, had actively participated in the uprisings and like so many disappointed German liberals, emigrated to America in 1849. Heinrich Engelhard Steinweg followed with his family in 1850.

Upon arriving in America, the father and sons worked in a piano factory. The father founded Steinway & Sons on March 5, 1853. The first factory was located at 81 Walker Street, in Manhattan, and was moved in 1859 to Park Avenue at 53rd Street, the present site of the Seagrams Building, where it covered a whole block. All the children, with the exception of Christian Friedrich Theodor, who had remained in Germany, worked in the business.

The firm prospered swiftly. "One of the most important improvements introduced by the Steinways was the cross-shaped arrangement of the strings. They also built the first upright instrument (1866) which, since it required less space, displaced the square piano," writes Rudolf Cronau ("Three Centuries of German Life in America").

In 1865, Theodor Steinweg came to America to help manage the family business, which shortly afterwards moved to Astoria, Long Island City, where it now comprises an enormous complex on Steinway Street.

The founder, Heinrich Steinway, died on February 7, 1871, in New York.

The Steinways were not and are not only pianobuilders. Even during the lifetime of the founder, they played an important role in the cultural life of their new homeland. In 1866, they founded Steinway Hall on 14th Street. The acoustics were excellent, and the hall, the predecessor of Carnegie Hall, seated 2000.

The Steinways did not forget their old homeland. For several years the branch offices which they established in Hamburg and Berlin have held piano competitions for young people, following the example of Steinway in New York. The management of the business is now in the hands of three Steinway brothers—John, Theodore, and Henry.

Friedrich Wilhelm von Steuben

Baron Friedrich Wilhelm August Heinrich Ferdinand von Steuben, Inspector General of the American army during the War of Independence, a former Prussian captain and temporary adjutant of Frederick the Great, was born September 17, 1730, in Magdeburg. George Washington needed experienced officers, and Steuben came to America at the suggestion of Benjamin Franklin, whom he met in Paris. Franklin was familiar with the military and organizational talents of Steuben, who fought at Rossbach and elsewhere during the Seven Years War.

Steuben landed in Portsmouth, New Hampshire on December 1, 1777, "as an exponent of the feelings characteristic of Prussia, its king, and its educated classes," according to Foreign Minister Gustav Stresemann in a speech commemorating the 150th anniversary of this date. But he was later to become an exponent of democracy.

Steuben found desolate conditions in Washington's winter quarters at Valley Forge. Only a few thousand men had remained loyal, supplies were inadequate, and the troops were decimated by desertions and corruption. Steuben was quickly able to overcome the soldiers' antagonism toward a foreigner ("he couldn't even curse in English"). He rose early every morning and drilled the soldiers himself, which was something officers had never done before. He swiftly comprehended the difference between the soldiers from the militia and those who had been pressed into service. "The genius of the American nation cannot be compared with that of Prussia, Austria, or France. In Europe a soldier is told what to do and he does it, but here I have to explain to the soldier why he should do it, and he will then do it."

Steuben was able to blend Prussian discipline with the backwoods fighting tactics that had proved so successful in the Indian wars. At the Battle of Monmouth on June 28, 1778, which brought a turning point in the war, "the reorganized continental army was able to pass the first test, after which it showed itself on a par with the best regular English troops," according to Admiral Samuel Eliot Morrison in his "Oxford History of the American People."

In the army regulations formulated by him that remained in effect for many decades, Steuben stresses, "a captain can never be too conscientious in his concern for his company entrusted to him by the state ... He must regard the devotion of his troops as his highest

FRIEDRICH WILHELM VON STEUBEN

goal by treating them with all possible friendship and humanity ... ''
This too was a new tone.

The professional officer who had grown up in the service of the monarch became a convinced democrat. Steuben wrote to Germany in 1779 as follows: '' ... What a fortunate country this is! Without kings, without high priests, without bloodsucking leaseholders and without idle barons ... I want to die gladly for a nation that has so honored me with its trust ... ''

Steuben lived in New York where, as the long-time President of the German Society, he concerned himself with the improvement of the lot of German immigrants who were often brutally handled. He subsequently moved to his estate in Oneida, New York, which was given to him by the state. Other states also gave him land.

Steuben died in Oneida on November 25, 1794.

Levi Strauss

Blue jeans are the uniform of the ''blue international.'' They are worn on all continents wherever people get hold of them. In the Soviet Union, they are traded on the black market. No other article of clothing has so intensely preoccupied sociologists and philosophers. Scholars regard Levis, manufactured in San Francisco since 1850, either as ''a sociological phenomenon'' or ''symbolic of the desire to be 'in'.'' Others view Levis as the democratic symbol of the kind of freedom characteristic of California during the gold rush. Workers, students, housewives, princes and Arab sheiks wear them without giving too much thought to their symbolic function because, as one often hears, ''they are simply practical.''

Levi Strauss, an immigrant from Bavaria, would be surprised to read the scholarly discussions about his creation, but he would surely be glad that more than 800 million pairs of his pants have been sold to men and women since the time of his modest beginnings.

We do not know very much about him, only that he came from a modest family, that he wanted to get ahead. He was born in 1829, came to America at the age of 14, and lived with an uncle in Louisville, Kentucky, until he became infected with gold rush fever.

He traveled to New York, where his brothers Jonas and Louis were in the dry goods trade, and bought a supply of silk, cloth, and a few luxury items. In addition, on his way West, he took along a supply of canvas intended for the Conestoga Wagons made by German wheelwrights in Pennsylvania and used by many gold prospectors to cross the continent. Thus equipped, he sailed around Cape Horn. Before arriving in San Francisco, he had sold all his merchandise except for the canvas, which was to make his fortune.

A gruff old prospector chided young Strauss for not having brought along a supply of pants, because prospecting for gold was rough on pants. Strauss promply had a tailor make pants from the canvas. The pants sold like hotcakes and were soon known as "Levis." In 1853, Levi Strauss founded a trading company with his brothers in New York.

Since that time, nothing essential has changed in this "piece of national heritage," except that the Strauss Brothers soon switched from canvas to another strong type of cloth called "serge de Nimes," which soon was shortened to "denim."

Another prospector, Alkali Ike, was to play a role in the evolution of jeans. Each time he returned to the saloons of Virginia City, he complained to his tailor, Jacob W. Davis, of pockets torn from his habit of carrying nuggets in them, and asked why Davis couldn't make his pockets as strong as those in Strauss' Levis. Davis, tired of his customer's constant complaining, riveted the pockets together with copper wire. When Alkali Ike returned a few weeks later, the entire boom town expected to witness the usual drunken spectacle, but this time the gruff miner, instead of getting drunk immediately and going around through the tents cursing, went to his tailor to show him that his pockets had held together. Davis reported the incident to Strauss, who applied with Davis for a patent on July 5, 1872. The patent, number 139,121, was granted on May 20, 1873, the date regarded as the birthday of the firm.

Strauss, who never married, died in 1902. The sons of his brothers continued to direct the company, which today is among the world's largest textile corporations. Some of the early Levis are now in the Smithsonian Institute in Washington, D.C.

One final paradox. Levis Strauss abhorred the name "jeans" and in his advertisements always referred to "overalls."

Johann August Sutter

Johann August Sutter was born in Kandern in Baden on February 23, 1803. He was an adventurer and colonizer whose controversial role in the development of America is best characterized by a quotation from Schiller: "Confused by the favor or hatred of interested parties, his image vacillates through history."

General Sutter, as he was generally known, was forced to flee his creditors in Switzerland at the age of 30. Ten years later, in California, he was the "ruler of the Sacramento Valley, founder of New Helvetia, a small sovereign." After the discovery of gold on his land he lost everything. Gold was his ruin. He never recovered from the loss of his property.

More has been written about Sutter than about any other German-American (Sutter himself usually claimed to be German-Swiss). After decades of obscurity, several books about his life were published. The first of these, Blaise Cendrars "L'or; la merveilleuse histoire du general Johann August Sutter," appeared in 1925 and was a distorted biography that became the source for numerous subsequent literary treatments in German of Sutter's life. Among these are Stefan Zweig's "The Discovery of Eldorado," "Ballade of Fort Sutter," by Egon Erwin Kisch, and "The History of General Johann August Sutter" by Caesar von Arx. Bruno Frank's "The General and the Gold" was also based on Cendrars. E. W. Moeller, in his "California Tragedy," portrayed Sutter as a kind of crusader for his rights, while Arx depicted Sutter quite wrongly as a con-man and gambler.

In 1876, the well-known historian, Herbert H. Bancroft, visited Sutter, who was ill, to have him dictate his autobiography. Bancroft's corrected notes were used as the source for "New Helvetia — Memoirs of General Johann August Sutter," published by Erwin Gustav Gudde in Leipzig in 1934. Two years earlier, D. S. Watson had published "The Diary of Johann August Sutter" in San Francisco. Both works are considered reliable.

The historian Bancroft made the most objective assessment of Sutter's importance in American history. Civil War general, William T. Sherman, observed in his eulogy on Sutter that "of all the men who played a role in reaching California, we owe its permanent possession primarily to General Sutter."

In California, Sutter worked on cultivation of grains, crops that had been almost completely neglected due to lack of irrigation. The present prosperity of the Sacramento Valley is largely a result of his foresight.

Some dates in Sutter's life remain unclear. He lived for a while in the Swiss canton of Basel, served in the Swiss Army, was promoted to the rank of captain, incurred debts and had to flee. In 1826, he married Anna Duebel, and they had three sons and a daughter. In 1834, he came to New York. In the next few years, he joined trappers in Oregon, visited Vancouver and the Hawaiian Islands, but always was attracted by Eldorado, or California. In July of 1839, he arrived in San Francisco, where he soon made a fortune.

Only a few days after his arrival (California at that time still belonged to Mexico), he presented the Mexican Governor, Alvarado, with a bold plan for founding a colony in the unexplored north on the southern bank of the American River, where it joins the Sacramento River. The governor granted him a vast tract of land where Sutter planted orchards, vineyards and grain and began to build extensive irrigation projects. In June 1841, the governor visited Neuve Helvetio, as Sutter called his kingdom, and conferred Mexican citizenship upon him. The success of Sutter's enterprise was phenomenal. He was considered the richest and most respected citizen of California, and became known as General Sutter.

His fortune changed when nuggets of a yellow metal were found on his land by James W. Marshall in January 24, 1848. News of the discovery of gold quickly spread through the entire colony, despite Sutter's effort to keep the discovery a secret. All his men fled, and thousands of gold prospectors overran his land, destroying fields, harvest, buildings, and became squatters. Sutter, who salvaged little, fled. "Even my millstones were stolen," he later told Bancroft.

He spent the next years making petitions to the federal government in Washington, which granted him a modest pension. In 1864, the legislature of California also granted him a monthly stipend of $250. In 1871, he bought a house in Lititz, Pennsylvania, in the village of the Moravian Brothers. He continued to spend winters in Washington where he died on June 18, 1880.

Paul Johannes Tillich

The Protestant theologian and philosopher, Paul Johannes Tillich (born August 20, 1886 in Starzeddel, Brendenburg) "holds a special position in American Protestant thought, due to the originality and depth of his theological thinking. He and the brothers, Richard and Reinhold Niebuhr, are mainly responsible for the renewal of interest in Christian thinking in America." (Laura Fermi, "Illustrious Immigrants")

Tillich was an intellectual influence on two continents until the age of 80 and was even known in Japan. Time Magazine stressed that he was not only respected among his colleagues, but that "his name was better known among laymen than that of any other contemporary theologian. His lectures in America were oversubscribed, and his books (he wrote more than 20) were sold in paperback editions into the hundreds of thousands. There was good reason for this, because Tillich was untiring in his efforts to relate theology to the issues of our time."

"In order to accomplish this, Tillich had to live on the boundary between the holy and the profane," Dean Jerald Brauer of the Divinity School of the University of Chicago explained. He was preoccupied for many years with coming to terms with the concept of boundary, which was the topic of his acceptance speech in the Paulskirche in Frankfurt on September 23, 1962 on the occasion of winning the Peace Prize of the Association of German Publishers and Booksellers. He spoke on the border between country and state, between feudality and bureaucracy, between religion and culture, between theology and philosophy and, in a personal sense, between two continents.

Tillich was ordained in 1912 as pastor of the Lutheran Church in Halle, having completed his degree a year before in Breslau. During World War I, he served as a field chaplain. Among the dying soldiers, he often asked himself whether the God of the Bible still existed.

After the war, he taught at the universities of Berlin, Marburg, Dresden, and Leipzig. In Berlin he met the woman who was to become his second wife, Hannah Werner, who later described her life with Tillich from Berlin to Chicago in her autobiography, "From Time to Time." In 1933, while on the faculty of Frankfurt University, he published the book, "The Socialist Decision." He later remarked with a certain pride, "I had the honor of being the first

PAUL TILLICH

non-Jewish professor to be expelled from a German university.''

Tillich came to America with his family at the invitation of Reinhold Niebuhr, who was intellectually close to him. His first position was as a member of the faculty of Union Theological Seminary in New York. In 1954, he received a call from Harvard, which honored him by conferring upon him the unusual title of University Professor. After 1962, he taught at the University of Chicago.

He subsequently also taught at the New School for Social Research in New York, where he met many friends from Germany. He counselled his classes, ''Preserve your integrity and have the courage to say no, even when society exerts strong pressure on you ...'' Tillich repeatedly demonstrated his courage to say no, and he had the intellectual equipment for convincingly substantiating his reasons for saying no.

Tillich died on October 22, 1965, in Chicago. At funeral services held at the University of Frankfurt, Max Horkheimer said, ''Whoever associated with Paul Tillich experienced true friendship. Those who had anything to do with him knew that the coloration of his voice and his gestures, reminding one of theology or of a pastor, knew it was not superficiality or routine but was the true expression of his thinking and aspirations.''

𝔘niversity in 𝔈xile

Among the numerous contributions from the Federal Republic of Germany on the occasion of the bicentennial celebration of American independence was the endowment of the Theodor Heuss Chair for Social Sciences at the Graduate Faculty of the New School for Social Research in New York. One of the reasons for the endowment cited at the dedication ceremony was the special character of the school imparted by its faculty composed of German refugees after 1933.

What began as a haven for immigrants became an intellectual bridge between the academic life of America and of the Federal Republic. ''The New School was a place of refuge and a forum for the integration of scholars and intellectuals into the spiritual and cultural life of America,'' as Ambassador Berndt von Staden stressed at the dedication ceremonies in New York.

The University in Exile, established in October 1933, provided perhaps the most important bridge to the new Germany after the year 1945. The bridge has been symbolically strengthened by the permanent endowment of the Theodor Heuss Chair. Prior to its endowment, a Chair for prominent guest professors from the Federal Republic was established at the instigation of Theodor Heuss, former President of the Federal Republic, and was financed by the Volkswagen Foundation. Within the framework of the Graduate Faculty that emerged from the University in Exile, those who left Germany under the pressure of Nazism now work in closest contact with guest professors from the Federal Republic.

In 1933 and for years following, the University in Exile was popularly known in New York as Little Heidelberg on 12th Street. The New School became the first gathering point for the intellectual immigration from Europe. Dr. Alvin Johnson, President of the New School, was one of the first American scholars to realize what a dangerous influence totalitarian regimes could exert on academic freedom.

As editor of the Encyclopedia of Social Sciences, Dr. Johnson had come into contact with numerous European economists, psychologists, sociologists, and jurists, and with the University in Exile as a part of the New School, he created a new forum of influence for those among them who had to leave their homes.

"In the course of years, the New School admitted and employed an incredible number of refugees to give lectures in regular or special programs, sometimes permanently. Thus countless scholars, scientists, artists and musicians made their first encounters with American education and culture through the doors of the New School. Many Europeans owe their lives to Alvin Johnson," says Laura Fermi (widow of the famous atomic physicist, in her book, "The Illustrious Immigrants").

For its part, the New School regards the creation of the Graduate Faculty as the greatest collective accomplishment by the refugee scholars. The Graduate Faculty is a monument to the scholarly accomplishments of these refugees.

Space prohibits an enumeration of all the important personalities from Germany who exerted an influence on American cultural life through this institution, an influence that was recognized in all academic circles. To mention only a few persons of distinction: Hans Simons, son of the president of Germany's supreme court, became president of the New School and co-author of the Basic Law of the

64

Federal Republic; Arnold Brecht, one of the leading personalities of the Weimar Republic, wrote his fundamental work, "Political Philosophy," while teaching at the New School; Max Wertheimer became the main authority on Gestalt psychology in the United States; Hannah Arendt achieved worldwide recognition for her work in the social sciences. Other famous personalities who initiated German-American intellectual exchange were the economists Karl Brandt, Gerhard Colm, Emil Lederer (the first dean of the Graduate Faculty), Adolph Loewe, Hans Speier, and the former state secretary of the Prussian Ministry for Commerce and Industry, Hans Staudinger, who also became dean of the Graduate Faculty and still remains active as a leader in the intellectual dialogue between America and Germany.

Erwin Piscator, who later returned to Berlin, was also active at the New School, which placed at his disposal a drama workshop that trained famous American actors. Other personalities included Carl Zuckmayer and the conductor, Otto Klemperer. The list is endless.

Little Heidelberg on 12th Street became one of the most remarkable institutions of America, and its doors were always open to German scholars. By this the New School opened the doors to other American universities for German scholars in the years following 1933 and again after the war.

Henry Villard

Among the number of great American industrialists who opened up the continent through railway construction, Heinrich Gustav Hilgard (born in Speyer on April 10, 1835), who called himself Henry Villard, occupies a special place. Villard, who fought bitterly against some of the shrewdest entrepreneurs of his time, the Goulds and the Hills, was known for the considerate treatment of his construction crews, in contrast to their brutal exploitation by other operators. Carl Schurz wrote that "Villard, whom I got to know as an active and very far-sighted man, was also an enthusiastic idealist ... Among those who accumulated great wealth during the period of America's industrialization—and Villard did that—there were only few idealists."

Villard emigrated to America after the 1848/49 uprisings. His father, Gustav Leonhard Hilgard (his mother was the former Katharina Antonia Pfeiffer) held a high judicial post and was loyal to the government, while two of his uncles fought on the barricades. Young Heinrich had a dispute with his father and fled. Fearing that his father would have him brought back, he changed his name upon arriving in America. He landed in New York in October of 1853 and proceeded after a brief time to the Northwest. For the next few years he got by as best he could and learned to speak English without an accent. In 1858, the New York Staatszeitung employed him as a reporter. He wrote on the Lincoln-Douglas debates, which were to become crucial to Lincoln, and established friendly contacts with the future president. Anecdotes told by Lincoln and published by Villard attracted much attention.

A visit to the gold mining camps resulted in Villard's writing a book, "The Past and Present of the Pike's Peak Gold Regions" (1860) which contains a detailed description of Colorado's natural riches.

Several newspaper publishers began to notice the young journalist and he became a star reporter at the Republican Convention in Chicago in the same year his book was published. In addition to the New York Herald, he wrote for several Western papers; hence many of the news reports read throughout the country during those crucial weeks were written by a young immigrant who was not yet 25.

In the Civil War, he reported on the Union side and was a loyal follower of Lincoln. In the post-war period, he had an opportunity to study banking and finance. In 1871, health reasons forced him to travel to Germany and Switzerland. Here he organized German holders of bonds issued by the Oregon and Pacific railroad. He returned to America as their representative. He was so successful that German holders of Kansas-Pacific bonds also appointed him to be their American representative.

Villard soon enjoyed such a reputation for honesty that, when he tried to raise eight million dollars without disclosing for what purpose, he soon had $12 million at his disposal in one of the most remarkable achievements of railroad financing. Between 1879 and 1883, Villard was one of the most influential railroad entrepreneurs in the United States. He became the driving force behind the construction of the Northern Pacific Railroad, a vitally important link to the Northwest.

At the ceremony for the opening of the Northern Pacific Railroad he had invited famous artists, journalists, parlamentarians and financiers. During the celebration, he learned that a group of financiers, under the leadership of his archenemy Jack Gould, had engineered a devastating plunge in the value of stocks Gould controlled. As a result, Villard suffered a nervous breakdown. He recuperated in Germany and returned to America in 1887 as representative of German financial interests to reorganize the Oregon & Transcontinental. In 1888, he was reappointed to the board of the Northern Pacific. He then directed his interest to other areas, and with Edison founded Edison General Electric in 1889. As early as 1881, he had acquired controlling interest in the New York Evening Post. He appointed Carl Schurz as Editor-in-Chief and Horace White and E. L. Godkin as editors. The paper was unique in that its publisher never attempted to dictate editorial policy and that the three editors worked together without conflict.

Villard made large bequests in America and in Germany. His philanthropic activity served as an example to such magnates as Rockefeller and others.

On January 3, 1866, he had married Helen Francis, only daughter of the abolitionist William Lloyd Garrison. Mrs. Villard made an important contribution to the womens' suffrage movement, was an active member of the NAACP and founded the Women's Peace Society in 1919.

Henry Villard died on November 12, 1900, on his estate in Dobbs Ferry. The Villard houses on Madison Avenue and 50th Street in New York remain as evidence of his exquisite taste.

Robert Wagner

Champion of the underdog best describes the accomplishment of U.S. Senator Robert Wagner, who was born in Nastaetten/Hesse on June 8, 1877. His name is preserved in the Wagner Act, or the National Labor Relations Act of 1935, which may be called the Magna Charta of the United States labor unions. Much to Wagner's regret, the bill was later restricted somewhat by the Taft-Hartley legislation.

Wagner also was the architect of the Social Security System. "Your name is indissolubly tied to America's second Bill of Rights," declared President Franklin D. Roosevelt in 1944.

Wagner's parents immigrated to America in 1886. His father had difficulty earning a living in New York. He worked in Yorkville as a building superintendent for a free basement apartment and a

ROBERT WAGNER

weekly wage of $5. Bobby, the youngest of seven children, helped by delivering newspapers and groceries. His older brother, Gus, who worked as a cook for the New York Athletic Club, helped his talented younger brother who "always wanted to go to school" to study at New York's City College. In 1896, the disappointed parents returned to Nastaetten.

While attending school, Bob worked as a page. Bob also worked at the New York Athletic Club while attending law school. In 1900 he was admitted to the Bar in New York. During an impromptu debate in the Algonquin Democratic Club in Yorkville, he attracted the attention of politicians from the Tammany Hall. Four years later he was a member of the Albany legislature. His parliamentary ascent was steep. From 1908–1918 he served as New York State Senator, from 1911 as Minority Leader, and was Deputy Lieutenant Governor in 1914 for a few months. From the beginning of his parliamentary career, his goal was "to fulfill our social obligations." He was strengthened in his commitment by the disastrous fire in the Triangle Shirtwaist Company in New York on March 25, 1911, which killed 200 workers. From that date, Wagner fought untiringly, even though for a long time unsuccessfully, for safe working conditions, unemployment insurance, and restrictions on child labor. As a result of his activity, the Federation of Labor could announce in 1913 that New York State had the best labor laws in the U.S.

In 1919 Wagner was appointed Justice of the New York Supreme Court, and in 1926 he was elected to his first term in the U.S. Senate. "We are confronted with revolutionary changes in the industrial production which are as profound as those of the beginning of the last century," he warned. Year after year he introduced bills in support of job security, unemployment support, and old age pensions. When he was accused of being a socialist, he responded by asking whether it was socialism "if one tries to raise the standard of living in the interest of the commonweal?" In 1932, after some hard battles, he pushed through the Relief Construction Act, a law which "for the first time recognized the responsibility of the federal government for the unemployed."

When Franklin D. Roosevelt was elected President, Wagner became the "legislative pilot of the New Deal." Not all his dreams came true, however. A national health insurance system, for which he introduced a bill as early as 1939, still remains controversial.

During his lifetime it was written that "since the days of the founding fathers no legislator has realized more or introduced more revolutionary bills in America history." "Current Biography" noted in 1941 that "Wagner's activities in the Senate represent a history of progressive legislation in America." Wagner's fundamental honesty, humanitarian integrity, and dedication to his cause were never doubted.

In 1947, Robert F. Wagner resigned from his senate seat because of health considerations. He then lived in Islip, Long Island, during the summers and spent winters with his son, Robert F. Wagner, Jr., who served three terms as Mayor of New York City. Senator Wagner died on May 4, 1953. Shortly before his death he declared "We need new recruits for the army of progress and humanity. But history is on our side."

Bruno Walter

Bruno Walter, "one of the greatest German conductors of all time" (David Ewen: Living Musicians), died on February 17, 1962, in Beverly Hills, California. However, he is by no means forgotten today, as Harold C. Schonberg, the eminent music critic of the New York Times (January 4, 1976), stresses. He belonged to a group of German conductors that includes such personalities as Otto Klemperer, Fritz Busch, Erich Leinsdorf, and William Steinberg — men who fled Germany during the Nazi era and found in America a new sphere of activity that had a profound influence on American musical life.

Born in Berlin on September 15, 1876 (his full name was Bruno Walter Schlesinger), Walter called his life an odyssey, and remained in America "the especially revered interpreter . . . of the great tradition of German musical culture" (Lawrence Gilman). Like other European conductors, he concentrated on German music both in Europe and in America although he was completely at home with the repertoire of other countries.

As he wrote in his highly valuable autobiography, "Theme and Variations," his (final) resettling in America took place without crisis. He was completely "aware of the differences in tempo," which he had already registered during his first American guest appearances in the year 1923. He saw that in the meantime America's vitality had not diminished, but he did not need to relinquish any of his own self as a human being or as an artist. His own rhythm was, as Walter wrote, always determined by "the specific weight of my nature." He said: "I am less inclined egocentrically than may be good for asserting myself ... My inclination is to sympathize with others."

Walter derived his great inner strength from his ability to sympathize. It enabled him to lead his musicians and singers without the trappings of stardom or mannerisms. "His deeply poetic talent, his superb musical intellect, his ability to achieve performances of great animation and wealth of feeling, gained him admiration" (Ewen) as early as January 13, 1932, when he returned to America after an absence of several years.

Walter was an artist of extraordinary versatility. He was at home in the concert hall and at the opera. He was a composer whose work includes, among other things, two symphonies, song albums, and piano quintets. In addition to the autobiography, which also provides a picture of German and European history, he published "Concerning the Moral Strength of Music" (1935) and "Of Music and Music Making" (1957). In 1941, he wrote a book on Gustave Mahler, in tribute to the composer, whom he had first met when he was 18.

Walter at that time had just completed the first stages of his odyssey. Coming from poor circumstances, he had had to struggle to be able to study at the Stern Conservatory in Berlin. Afterwards, he held a minor position at the Cologne Opera House. Working under Mahler became decisive for his entire development. Mahler encouraged the young man, who had not yet found himself, and Walter never forgot that. Throughout his life Walter was a pioneer in performing Mahler's work. Mahler had had difficulty in succeeding during his own lifetime and remained, for the most part, unknown in America for a long time. After Mahler's death, Walter was the first to conduct his "Lied von der Erde" and his Ninth Symphony (1912). Walter conducted in Riga, at the Royal Opera in Berlin, and at the Royal Opera in Vienna when Mahler also conducted there "in that decade whose heights were rarely reached before or since" (Current Biography, 1942).

Upon Mahler's death in 1911, his post in Vienna was filled by Walter. Two years later, however, Walter assumed the direction of the Royal Opera House in Munich, where he remained for ten years and where he was also responsible for the Munich Music Festivals. He was everywhere in demand—in Barcelona, Stockholm, Warsaw, Moscow, Budapest, Prague.

His Mozart summer concerts in Salzburg set new standards. He also performed as a pianist. The piano was the only instrument that he completely mastered (for as he once said, he did not want just to half-learn other instruments). From 1925–29 he was musical director of the City Opera in Berlin-Charlottenburg. In 1929 he succeeded Furtwaengler at the Leipzig Gewandhaus. Then came the period at the Concertgebouw in Amsterdam, a period of time in Salzburg and Vienna, and emigration to France, which conferred French citizenship on him, a rare distinction for refugees.

Then came the emigration to America. He established himself in California, became guest director of the NBC Symphony Orchestra, and was guest director and consultant of the New York Philharmonic.

His debut at the Metropolitan Opera took place on February 14, 1941, when he conducted a performance of "Fidelio" that entered the annals of opera history. This was followed by additional performances at the Met and in other American cities from New York to Los Angeles. Walter did not have his own orchestra, but as Laura Fermi explains in "Illustrious Immigrants," through his concerts and rehearsals he influenced the musical understanding and interpretations of countless American musicians.

He remained hearty and active into his old age (he died at 85). During his lifetime he founded the Bruno Walter Memorial Foundation with his own funds. In an article by Schonberg entitled "The Conductor as Saint," the critic calls Walter "the conscience of music — he regarded music as a spiritual power — he was the high priest who proclaimed its message . . ."

Kurt Weill

Kurt Weill, the composer of the "Three Penny Opera," whom the American press time and again writes about as the embodiment of Berlin's "Golden Twenties," "was able," as Leonard Bernstein said, "to transplant the impetuosity of his German training, and his expressionistic-intellectual past to Broadway." Weill wrote operas and songs which today are remembered as "classic Americana." His short opera, "Down in the Valley," rooted in the folklore of the American West, is staged year after year by American college theater groups. His "September Song" (from "Knickerbocker Holiday") has become a true American classic.

Weill believed in the mass appeal of music, but he never lowered his standards. In America, too, his thoughts were filled by the theory of "contemporary opera." Nothing was too daring for Weill. His musicals had themes that were as unpopular as war, dictatorship, racism, slums, corruption. Weill, a highly sensitive musician, student of Ferrucio Busoni, one of the few composers who did his own orchestrations, was also a full-blooded man of the theater. That helped him in the adjustment from Berlin to Broadway.

Born in Dessau on March 2, 1900, Weill came from a musically-inclined family. His father, Albert, was cantor of his synagogue, his mother an amateur pianist. After brief studies at the Academy of Music in Berlin, Weill was drawn to the theater, where he worked as choirmaster for several houses. In 1921, he started to study under Busoni. Originally a member of the twelve-tone school, he began to look for a new mode of expression of "music for this time," which would be capable of gripping its audience. His first short surrealistic opera "The Protagonist," (libretto by Georg Kaiser), which premiered on March 27, 1926, at the Staatsoper in Dresden under Fritz Busch, already earned him some fame. His satirical jazz-style opera "Der Zar laesst sich photographieren" was given by 80 German theaters.

With the "Three Penny Opera" (first performed in the Theater at the Schiffbauerdamm on August 31, 1928) Weill became known throughout the musical world. This vehement piece, which takes place in John Gay's London but reflects turbulent Berlin of Weill's era—and which also made Weill's wife, Lotte Lenya, famous—was given more than 10,000 performances in Central Europe alone.

"Der Jasager" (The Yes-Man), "Die Bürgschaft" (The Pledge) and "Der Silbersee" (Silver Lake) followed quickly; the latter in several theaters in February 1933, even after Hitler's seizure of power.

Then Weill had to flee. Paris received him with open arms. There he created the ballet for voice and orchestra, "The Seven Mortal Sins," for the dancer Tilly Losch. Max Reinhardt invited him to come to America to write the music for Franz Werfel's biblical drama "The Eternal Road." As Reinhardt encountered problems during the production, Weill first composed the music for the anti-war opera "Johnny Johnson," written by Paul Green, the author of numerous, repeatedly performed symphonic dramatizations of American history, whom Weill had met in Berlin. "Johnny Johnson" is the satirical and melancholy history of a disappointed soldier returning from the war.

Weill once said, "Since I came to America I dreamed of American opera." And so he looked for American material. "Knicker-

73

bocker Holiday'' (1938) brought the old, small, Dutch New Amsterdam, Peter Stuyvesant, the ancestors of Franklin D. Roosevelt, political intrigue and corruption to the Broadway stage. "A hit," a critic wrote. "The gentlemen of Broadway should be careful. Weill proved that the old over-used formulas no longer draw the public." Broadway had "a new man."

Weill worked unceasingly. Melodies just came to him, well-known writers sent him plays, producers fought for him. Hollywood made some of his musicals into films, but he remained faithful to the theater. He had arrived at the conviction that the new American opera would find its origins in the musical — the Broadway musical. That was to be confirmed after his death. Some of his musicals found their way to the stages of American opera houses.

He was never satisfied with what he had achieved. He hated stereotypes, as he had in Berlin. He never repeated himself. "Lady in the Dark" was a "psychoanalytic" musical about a dream fantasy with a script by Moss Hart and lyrics by Ira Gershwin. In 1972, the prominent critic Lehman Engel said that this was the only musical that had remained young. Together with Ogden Nash he wrote "One Touch of Venus," based on the ancient legend of Galatea.

Weill called his "Street Scene" of 1947 a "dramatic musical." It is truly an opera. Weill found the material in the drama of the same name by Elmer Rice, an admirer of the German Expressionists. The locale: a large apartment house in Manhattan, and its colorful mix of tenants which no melting pot can bring together. For the prominent music critic, Olin Downes, "Street Scene" was "the most crucial step towards an American opera that was undertaken in a Broadway theater." Bernhard Gruen called the musical "a passionate-realistic popular drama — a white Porgy and Bess."

Weill's last musical, "Lost in the Stars" (based on an adaptation of Alan Paton's "Cry, the Beloved Country," which takes place in South Africa) is an indictment of racism. "Weill brought the play up to the high level of a spiritual experience," wrote Brooks Atkinson, the dean of New York critics.

Weill died near New York on April 3, 1950, only 50 years old.

Friedrich Weyerhaeuser

Friedrich Weyerhaeuser (born in 1834 in Niedersaulheim, Rhein-Hesse), became one of "the giants of American business life" (Cronau: "Three Centuries of German Life in America"). He created an empire in lumbering and saw mills and his influence extended to other areas of the economy. His sons and grandsons further expanded the Weyerhaeuser fortune.

Weyerhaeuser was known as the Timber King, a title he disliked thoroughly. He remained throughout his life a simple man who shied away from publicity. In this respect, he resembled John Jacob Astor with whom he is often compared. Because of his retiring nature, his name is not to be found in the Dictionary of American Biographies, in contrast to other industrial magnates. Even Who's Who in America discovered him only in 1911, three years before his death. He enjoyed his anonymity, as did his descendants who, in contrast to the founder of the dynasty, won degrees at colleges and universities.

Friedrich's parents, Johann and Katherine (born Gaebel) were wine growers in their home town (they had approximately 15 acres). His father died at age 52, when Friedrich was not yet 12 years old. A year later he had to leave school and tend the farm. Of 11 children, only he and four of his sisters survived.

Like so many poor people from Germany, Friedrich Weyerhaeuser came to America in the wake of the unsuccessful uprisings of 1848–49, in which he had not taken an active part. For a while he worked as a day laborer in the vicinity of Erie, Pennsylvania, where he married Elisabeth Bladel. He then moved to Rock Island, Illinois, and worked on a railroad. He was also a carter. A quiet, shy person who kept his eyes open, he quickly comprehended the realities of America, and laughed good-naturedly when his fellow workers teased him about his thick Hessian accent and mispronounced his name.

He advanced quickly wherever he worked. In one of the few interviews he ever gave, when asked to explain the reasons for his tremendous success, he said, "The secret lay simply in my will to work. I never watched the clock and never stopped before I had finished what I was working on."

His bosses entrusted him with the direction of a sawmill in Rock Island, and here he learned what was to become decisive for his

FRIEDRICH WEYERHAUSER

career. He was then put in charge of a timber yard in Coal Valley. When the company was ruined in the panic of 1857, Weyerhaeuser was able to acquire the timber yard and the sawmill with the little money he had saved. Soon afterwards, he bought logs from the shores of the Mississippi and acquired additional sawmills.

In the year 1864, Weyerhaeuser began to buy up pine tracts in upper Chippewa Valley, Wisconsin, after which he had all stages of the lumber business under his control. The bitterness of his competitors led to many timber wars, but by 1880, Weyerhaeuser emerged the winner. "He never was involved in bribery scandals..." (Richard G. Lillard: "Timber King"—The Pacific Spectator, Vol. 1, No. 1).

He acquired still more land in Wisconsin, Minnesota, Idaho, Washington, and Oregon. In 1891, he moved to St. Paul where, despite his practiced reticence, he played an active role in the community, especially in German-American circles. His friendship with James J. Hill "the small giant, the king of the Northern Pacific, Kaiser of the Berlington and a legendary figure" (Stewart H. Holbrook: American Railroads), was extremely valuable to him.

Hill had acquired millions of acres of the best timber forests cheaply from the government for his railroad. He knew nothing about the lumber business, however, and at a time when speculative lumbering often assumed the form of robbery, a practice against which Carl Schurz fought energetically, Weyerhaeuser recognized the industrial value of timberland. Since he professed not to work for himself but for his grandchildren, he tried to think of how he could acquire more timber forests. In time, he bought three million acres of forests from Hill.

By this time, the Weyerhaeuser Syndicate owned a large part of the Western section of the state of Washington, as well as vast stretches of land in Oregon and elsewhere. To his contemporaries and to the press, with which he did not concern himself, he remained the "mysterious man ... it is astonishing that such enormous wealth could be acquired without the public's knowing anything about it..." (Charles Norcross in Cosmopolitan Magazine, 1906). Gustavus Myers, in "The Great American Fortunes," holds the slightly malicious view that "Weyerhaeuser had a special talent for amassing millions in utter silence ..."

At the turn of the century, he owned more timberland than any other American (R.G. Lillard). He held rather liberal views, considering the period, and he showed greater concern for his workers than any other industrial magnate of the time. He impressed upon them the necessity of protecting even the smallest trees. He remained unassuming and quite well-liked by the woodsmen. He built himself a villa next door to his friend, James J. Hill. When the National German American Bank was in difficulties in 1893, he made it solvent again within a few months.

Upon his death on November 29, 1911, Hill commented, ''His place can never be filled... He was one of those national forces that helped build our country...''

John Peter Zenger

American journalism still pays tribute to John Peter Zenger (born in the Palatinate in 1697) as one of the first champions of freedom of the press. Zenger came to America at the age of 13. After devastations and famine his family, like many others from the Palatinate, had fled to Holland and then to England, from where Queen Anne sent them to America in 1710. Zenger's father died in the crowded steerage and his mother, Johanna, a younger brother and a sister had to indenture themselves to pay the costs of the passage. Peter was fortunate. He went into the service of William Bradford, a Quaker printer, who treated him decently and trained him well. Peter soon became his assistant and later his partner.

In 1726 Zenger opened his own shop on New York's Broad Street, printing some books, mostly in Dutch, and some polemic pamphlets. He felt himself drawn to the People's Party, which had been founded by another German immigrant, Vice Governor Jacob Leisler who was executed in 1691. The People's Party found itself in opposition to Governor William Cosby, who had arbitrarily dismissed Justice Lewis Morris, replacing him with his stooge James DeLancey. Governor Cosby had wanted Morris to recognize his completely unjustified claims for greater payments from government funds and to grant to himself and his family land in the Mohawk Valley, to which neither the Governor nor the members of his family had any claim. Morris had refused and had been pushed aside. Among the people of New York, the discontent about the arbitrary actions of the government was at the pitch as it was during Leisler's period. At that time, Leisler had become the spokesman of the opposition; now in 1735, it was Zenger. Together with Morris, James

Alexander and William Smith, he founded the New York Weekly Journal on November 5, 1733.

From the beginning, Zenger attacked nepotism and corruption in government. He made his newspaper available to his political friends and also wrote courageous and well-researched articles himself. As printer, he was responsible for the paper's entire content. A witch-hunt started—even his old master Bradford wrote against him in the New York Gazette, the government's voice. A few issues of Zenger's paper were ordered to be publicly burned. But the official who was to do it, cognizant of the popular mood, refused. The task was then given to the sheriff, who delegated it to a Negro slave. The latter could not refuse.

On November 17, 1734, Zenger was thrown into jail. Now his energetic wife, the former Anna Catherina Maul, became active. She visited him daily, even though she could only talk to him through a peephole in his cell door. Undeterred, she published further issues of the Journal.

When the trial started on August 4, 1735, it was considered a foregone conclusion that Zenger would be harshly sentenced. After all, Zenger had asserted that land records had been destroyed, judges arbitrarily dismissed and bribes paid, all by order of the Governor. According to the legal practice of the time, the jury merely had to decide whether the defendant had actually printed the document that had been declared seditious, not whether it really was libelous. Proof that the allegations were true was inadmissable.

De Lancey, who presided over the trial, had already prepared the verdict. But Zenger's friends, after the Court had rejected attorneys from New York, had engaged the highly-respected 80-year-old Andrew Hamilton from Philadelphia as attorney for the defense. He forced the court to go beyond formalistic law and the trial became "a part of American folklore." Hamilton was prepared to prove the truth of the allegations. De Lancey neither would nor could allow that, since he himself was involved. "This case," Hamilton declared in his final argument,"is not that of a simple printer,and not one that is of importance only to New York. It affects every free citizen in America. What is at stake is the highest of all human goods — liberty." To the dismay of the officials and the joy of the public, the jury brought in a verdict of "not guilty."

This was the first step toward new legislation in England, which culminated with the adoption of Fox's Libel Act by the London Parliament in 1792. Zenger himself had already died on July 28,

1746. In 1737, New York had gratefully appointed him public printer. But Zenger's family always had to contend with financial woes. His widow published his paper until 1748. It was continued by his son John until 1751.

Selective Bibliography

Adams, Willi Paul. **The German-Americans. An Ethnic Experience.** Trans. & adapted by LaVern J. Rippley and Eberhard Reichmann. (Indianapolis: Max Kade German-American Center, Indiana University-Purdue University, 1993)

Baxter, Angus. **In Search of Your German Roots: A Complete Guide to Tracing Your Ancestors in the Germanic Areas of Europe.**
(Baltimore: Genealogical Publishing Co., 1994)

Galicich, Anne. **The German-Americans.**
(New York: Chelsea House, 1989)

Haller, Charles R. **Distinguished German-Americans.**
(Bowie, MD: Heritage Books, 1995)

O'Connor, Richard. **The German-Americans: An Informal History.**
(Boston: Little, Brown & Co., 1968)

Rippley, LaVern J. **The German-Americans.**
(Lanham, MD: University Press of America, 1984)

Rippley, LaVern J. **Of German Ways.**
(Minneapolis: Dillon, 1970)

Tolzmann, Don Heinrich, ed. **German Achievements in America: Rudolf Cronau's Survey History.**
(Bowie, MD: Heritage Books, 1995)

Tolzmann, Don Heinrich. **German-Americana: A Bibliography.**
(Bowie, MD: Heritage Books, 1995)

Wust, Klaus. **Three Hundred Years of German Immigrants in North America, 1683-1983. A Pictorial History with 510 Illustrations.**
(Baltimore/Munich: Heinz Moos, 1983)

GERMAN-AMERICAN HERITAGE MAP (1990)
WHERE GERMAN-AMERICANS LIVE*

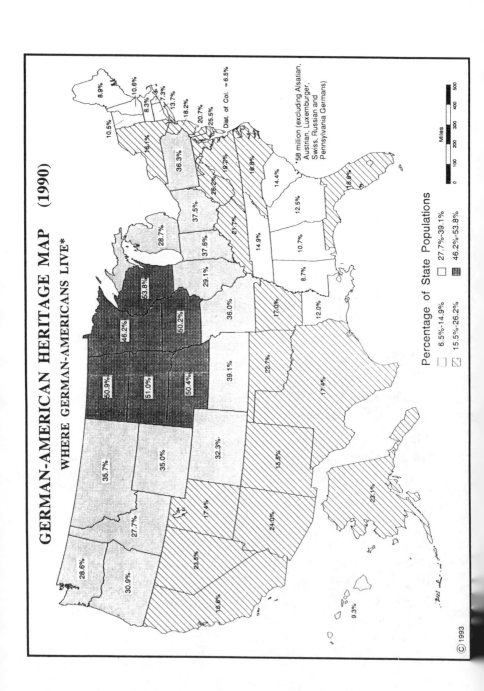

*58 million (excluding Alsatian, Austrian, Luxemburger, Swiss, Russian and Pennsylvania Germans)

Dist. of Col. = 6.5%

Percentage of State Populations

- 6.5%-14.9%
- 15.5%-26.2%
- 27.7%-39.1%
- 46.2%-53.8%

Miles

0   100   200   300   400   500

© 1993

German-American Census Statistics

States	Total Population	German Pop.	% by State	% of Total
United States	248,709,873	57,947,374	23.30%	23.30%
California	29,760,021	4,935,147	16.58%	1.98%
Pennsylvania	11,881,643	4,314,762	36.31%	1.73%
Ohio	10,847,115	4,067,840	37.50%	1.64%
Illinois	11,430,602	3,326,248	29.10%	1.34%
Texas	16,986,510	2,949,686	17.36%	1.19%
New York	17,990,455	2,898,888	16.11%	1.17%
Michigan	9,295,297	2,666,179	28.68%	1.07%
Wisconsin	4,891,769	2,630,680	53.78%	1.06%
Florida	12,937,926	2,410,257	18.63%	.97%
Indiana	5,544,159	2,084,667	37.60%	.84%
Minnesota	4,375,099	2,020,975	46.19%	.81%
Missouri	5,117,073	1,843,299	36.02%	.74%
New Jersey	7,730,188	1,407,956	18.21%	.57%
Iowa	2,776,755	1,394,542	50.22%	.56%
Washington	4,866,692	1,389,914	28.56%	.56%
Maryland	4,781,468	1,218,257	25.48%	.49%
Virginia	6,187,358	1,186,056	19.17%	.48%
North Carolina	6,628,637	1,110,581	16.75%	.45%
Colorado	3,294,394	1,063,694	32.29%	.43%
Kansas	2,477,574	968,078	39.07%	.39%
Oregon	2,842,321	878,555	30.91%	.35%
Arizona	3,665,228	878,088	23.96%	.35%
Georgia	6,478,216	810,165	12.51%	.33%
Kentucky	3,685,296	798,001	21.65%	.32%
Nebraska	1,578,385	794,911	50.36%	.32%
Tennessee	4,877,185	724,059	14.85%	.29%
Oklahoma	3,145,585	714,184	22.70%	.29%
Louisiana	4,219,973	507,453	12.03%	.20%
South Carolina	3,486,703	500,089	14.34%	.20%
Massachusetts	6,016,425	497,462	8.27%	.20%
West Virginia	1,793,477	468,927	26.15%	.19%
Connecticut	3,287,116	450,247	13.70%	.18%
Alabama	4,040,587	430,442	10.65%	.17%
Arkansas	2,350,725	400,234	17.03%	.16%
South Dakota	696,004	355,102	51.02%	.14%
North Dakota	638,800	324,923	50.87%	.13%
Utah	1,722,850	299,414	17.38%	.12%
Montana	799,065	285,385	35.71%	.11%
Nevada	1,201,833	279.693	23.27%	.11%
Idaho	1,006,749	278,615	27.67%	.11%
New Mexico	1,515,069	234,000	15.44%	.09%
Mississippi	2,573,216	224,674	8.73%	.09%
Wyoming	453,588	158,469	34.94%	.06%
Delaware	666,168	138,128	20.73%	.06%
Alaska	550,043	127,103	23.11%	.05%
New Hampshire	1,109,252	118,003	10.64%	.05%
Maine	1,227,928	108,859	8.87%	.04%
Hawaii	1,108,229	102,714	9.27%	.04%
Rhode Island	1,003,464	73,425	7.32%	.03%
Vermont	562,758	59,090	10.50%	.02%
District of Columbia	606,900	39,218	6.46%	.02%
Total Statistics	248,709,873	57,947,374	23.30%	23.30%